Table of Contents

Section One: The View from 30,000 Feet

To tip the odds in our favor, we need to understand these four subjects:

1. Self-knowledge: identifying our interests, talents, strengths and weakness

2. The emerging economy

3. The changing nature of work

4. The role of lifelong learning

Gaining self-knowledge is well-covered by the existing shelf of career counseling books such as *What Color Is Your Parachute?* and *Finding Your Way to Your Authentic Career*. As a result, I am setting that topic aside with the comment that it helps to distinguish between what you think you should do based on others' expectations, and what kinds of work actually align with your personality, your sources of fulfillment and the skills that create the most value. Choosing a path based on others' expectations is a good way to lose yourself and end up unhappy, and pursuing supposedly sure-things (such as getting a law degree or other advanced degree) are equally prone to disappointment.

I will address one aspect of self-knowledge in Section Five: getting clear about your beliefs about money and success.

We'll begin with an overview (the view from 30,000 feet) and then cover the three subjects in depth.

Later sections will lay out a practical guide to putting this knowledge to work in getting a job, establishing a livelihood and building a career. This will include the advances in behavioral economics and psychology that provide insights into the day-to-day practicalities of building a career.

The Changing Economy

The economy is unstable for a number of structural reasons, and this instability is not going to go away any time soon. Though we have been taught that the economy cycles between growth and recession—what's known as the business cycle—the growth of the past decade has been uneven at best. Beneath the surface, the economy is changing in fundamental ways that are confounding policy-makers mired in conventional thinking.

Some parts of the economy are shrinking because they are obsolete and fatally inefficient. Other parts are expanding because they are far more efficient than what they're replacing. There are in effect two economies mixed together, and the first step for anyone seeking a livelihood is to realize that opportunities in the shrinking sectors will be considerably fewer than those in the expanding sectors.

To understand why some sectors are declining and others are rising, we need to understand the basic machinery of capitalism and economics. Those who expect this to be painful may be pleasantly surprised at how quickly we'll cover these fundamentals.

As a result of technology, the nature of work is also changing rapidly. The shrinking sectors will still offer conventional jobs, but as technology leapfrogs the obsolete and inefficient, even these traditional jobs will be changing. Those who can't adapt to the new modes of work (or choose not to) will be left behind.

In the conventional view, a college degree prepares one to enter the workforce. This is no longer true, as higher education has failed to keep pace with technology and a fast-changing economy. Anyone seeking a livelihood must also understand the new role of education in the emerging economy.

Technology is disruptive, and what it will disrupt next is not easily predictable. But we can predict one aspect of disruption: technology will disrupt the most expensive sectors of the economy because that's where the greatest efficiencies and reductions in cost can be reaped.

In advanced economies, the costliest sectors are healthcare, education, government and national security/defense. Traditionally, these have long been considered stable sectors with guaranteed job security. Ironically, that is changing, as the soaring costs of these sectors now exceed the economy's ability to fund them.

If an economy expands by 2% each year and healthcare costs rise by 10% each year, eventually healthcare runs out of oxygen—there isn't enough income generated by the economy to fund its continued expansion.

In other words, the disruption of sectors with fast-rising costs is guaranteed. What this means for jobseekers is the traditional sources of job security are precisely the sectors that will be disrupted the most as costs will brought down as a matter of necessity: either costs will be controlled on the nation slips into insolvency.

How does an inefficient agency or enterprise cut costs? Since the largest expense for the vast majority of organizations is labor, the only way to make a significant impact on costs is to shed employees.

Whether we like it or not, enterprises don't have profits, they only have expenses. This insight by management author Peter Drucker helps us understand why it's so difficult to get a job: every employee is an expense, and the profits needed to keep the company financially viable are always uncertain.

While government agencies don't have profits, government depends on the profitability of private enterprise for taxes. A business can only afford to pay employees if it is viable, i.e. makes a profit. Companies that don't make a profit lose money and close their doors; unprofitable businesses vanish, along with their payroll and the taxes paid by the company and its employees.

Governments get around this dependence on profitable enterprises for tax revenues by borrowing money. The government borrows money by selling bonds: in exchange for a sum of cash, the government promises to return the buyer's cash at a later time with interest.

Borrowing money requires paying interest, which means that some portion of income is siphoned off to pay the annual interest. The more you borrow, the larger the slice of your income that goes to pay interest on your debt. If your income doesn't grow faster than interest payments, eventually all your income goes to pay interest and you have nothing left to live on.

This is called insolvency, and the only way out of insolvency is to declare bankruptcy and wipe out all the debt you owe.

That debt was a liability to you, but it was an asset to the lender. The buyer of the bond gave the government cash for the bond. If the government defaults and doesn't return the cash, the bond owner's asset is wiped out. That means the cash is no longer available to invest in something else. The default doesn't just harm the bond owner; it harms the economy because it reduces the capital available for productive investment.

This is important because anyone seeking a job or career has to understand that there is no free lunch in the long-term. Government, enterprises and households can borrow money to fund their expenses for a while, but eventually the interest catches up with them, and they go broke as the interest soaks up so much of their revenues that there's not enough left to pay essential bills.

Living off borrowed money is a fool's solution to rising costs. Eventually, income and expenses must align.

The point of this brief economics lesson is simple: the problems in our economy cannot be solved by financial trickery or by borrowing more money. Everyone, from individuals to households to companies to governments must eventually live within their means. The longer one lives beyond one's means with borrowed money, the more violent the re-alignment will be.

We have lived in an economy that depends on debt (borrowed money) and rising consumption for so long that we imagine this is always how it has been and how it will always be. Both assumptions are wrong. The shift away from debt-based consumption as the source of economic growth is inevitable, and this will have a profound impact on jobs and the nature of work.

In addition to these basic financial limits on debt and consumption, there are also limits imposed by demographics, resources and the environment. The workforce of most nations is ageing as people live longer and fewer children are born per family, placing greater financial burdens on the working age populace to fund the pensions and healthcare costs of a rapidly expanding elderly population. In response, people are working longer, but societies with costly pensions and healthcare systems are facing a widening gap between the numbers of people who are working full-time and paying taxes and those drawing retirement benefits.

Once the ratio of full-time workers to retirees drops to two workers to each retiree, it becomes financially impossible to fund the costs of retirement without taking most of the workers' wages as taxes. This sets up a politically unresolvable generational conflict.

In the U.S., we are already at that threshold: as of 2013, there were 57 million Social Security beneficiaries and only 114 million full-time workers.

Resources are being depleted and what is being extracted is rising in cost. Global fisheries, for example, are in a steep decline as the world's fishing fleets stripmine the seas. Even those who maintain that there is still plenty of oil and natural gas concede that the cheap, easy-to-get oil has been consumed; it now takes extraordinarily expensive measures to discover and extract deep oil. Extracting, refining and shipping hydrocarbon fuels now require more energy. The EROEI—energy return on energy invested—is declining. This means it now takes much more capital (investment of money) and energy to extract the same number of barrels of oil than it did in the past.

The environment is also under pressure as billions of people in developing economies pursue a high-consumption middle-class lifestyle.

Freshwater aquifers are being drained, imperiling the sustainability of agriculture and urban centers, and soil depletion and air quality have declined precipitously in many heavily populated regions.

For all these reasons, the assumption that rapidly rising debt and consumption are sustainable is false. This realization has given rise to a new understanding of the economy called Degrowth (French: *décroissance*, Spanish: *decrecimiento*, Italian: *decrescita*). I will have more to say on Degrowth later, but for now we need only grasp the core concept that expansion of consumption fueled by debt is qualitatively and quantitatively different from sustainable growth.

This runs counter to the conventional wisdom that growth of debt-based consumption is not only good, but it's the only possible path to prosperity.

From the perspective of sustainable prosperity, growth based on debt-based consumption is the road to ruin, as the foundations of fast-rising debt and ever-greater consumption are crumbling.

This shift from debt-based consumption to a more productive sustainability is bringing profound changes to the nature of work itself and social arrangements in the workplace.

The advancing capabilities of technology have replaced many kinds of jobs, and there is no end in sight for this trend of automation, robotics and software replacing human workers. This has led author Jeremy Rifkin to declare that advanced economies are approaching *The End of Work*.

This reduction in the need for human labor means the income side of consumption is also threatened: even if there were limitless fisheries, fresh water, energy, etc., the income needed to fund middle-class levels of consumption is being pressured by the replacement of human labor with machines and software.

The social ramifications of this erosion of conventional full-time middle-class jobs are far-reaching. Stagnation in opportunities to work and earn (i.e. a financial recession) leads to *social recession*, a loss of opportunities for adulthood: a rewarding career, family, and a home of one's own. In a social recession, unemployed young people may be mired in adolescent narcissism, eschewing ambitions not just in work but in romance and marriage.

In summary, the notion that progress requires ever-higher levels of consumption, all funded by ever-rising levels of debt, has run aground on the reality of limited resources, the destructive consequences of ever-rising debt and the replacement of human labor with automation, robotics and software.

From 30,000 feet, it's clear the current system of defining progress as ever-higher levels of debt and consumption is no longer viable for a number of structural reasons.

We need to redefine progress as something sustainable: an economy that prospers with little to no debt and declining levels of consumption. Ultimately, the emerging economy is all about doing more with less, and creating value and solving problems with fewer resources. That's where the opportunities are expanding, and that's where the work will be.

The idea that happiness and fulfillment required ever more consumption was always flawed; it was a marketing ploy to sell more goods and services, not an idea grounded in psychology. The more we learn about happiness and fulfillment, the more apparent it becomes that family, community, meaningful work and networks of colleagues, collaborators and friends are the sources of happiness and fulfillment , not the accumulation of stuff: more expansive homes, more shoes, etc., turn out to have little impact on happiness or fulfillment.

As a result, understanding the economy also means understanding the changing nature of work and value creation.

Let's start with a quick overview of economics and why it matters.

Why Economics Matters to Jobseekers

What does economics have to do with my getting a job and building a career? The short answer is: *everything*. Every sector in the economy is described by Bob Dylan's line: *he not busy being born is busy dying*. Jobseekers who are blind to the difference between sectors that are being born and those that are dying run the risk of placing all their chips on a sector that's dying. The odds of getting a job in a shrinking sector are considerably less than getting a job in an expanding sector.

The classic example is the buggy-whip industry: at the turn of the 20th century, horse-drawn vehicles were the primary mode of personal transport. With the advent of gasoline-powered automobiles, all the industries related to horse-drawn buggies either transitioned to become part of the horseless carriage (auto) industry or they vanished.

Those entering the buggy-whip industry were entering a dying sector with no future.

It's also critical to understand the interplay of major economic forces such as central government (called *the state* in political science) control, globalization and monopolies/cartels. Major economic forces are reactions to some existing economic extreme that gained outsized influence in society or that benefited the few at the expense of the many.

For example, modern capitalism can be seen as a reaction to the inequality, lack of opportunity and stagnation of the feudal economy. When large corporations established monopolies that could set prices without regard to market forces in the early 20th century, the state (government) stepped in to limit the excessive power of monopolies.

When government regulations multiplied to the point that they choked off growth, a movement arose to pare back regulations and state control of markets (neoliberalism).

When home markets no longer offered prospects for high growth, companies sought overseas markets (globalization).

The point for those seeking a career is this: what's riding high at the moment may be poised to reverse, and what seems like a desert could be about to bloom.

Here's an example of this dynamic. Back in the early 20th century, there were hundreds of local beer breweries. When the Federal government imposed Prohibition in 1920, these were closed down. When Prohibition was repealed in 1933, alcohol was once again legal and breweries re-opened.

The competitive advantages of large companies (called economies of scale) became a dominant force in the U.S. economy starting in the war years of the 1940s, and a consolidation trend swept through the economy. Small local breweries were bought up by larger firms, and by the end of the 1970s, there were only a handful of corporate breweries in the U.S.

Anyone who wanted a career in a local micro-brewery looked out on a desert: there were no micro-breweries at all. But this extreme concentration of ownership and the limited choices that resulted (not to mention the limited quality of the product) sparked a reaction: the micro-brewery industry has flourished since the 1980s, and now hundreds of local micro-breweries are creating thousands of jobs and reinvigorating towns and urban neighborhoods.

Here's another example: the U.S. military. Back in the Cold War era, a majority of young males completed a few years of military service, as the Armed Forces required millions of people. The pay was low but just about anyone who could pass the physical was accepted.

As technology advanced and the transition to a volunteer force took hold, military service has changed radically. The military needs far fewer people to operate, and the demands on those serving are higher—and so is the pay.

For the past decade, healthcare has been expanding rapidly in the U.S., and virtually everyone believes that healthcare will continue to offer plentiful job opportunities as this expansion will certainly continue for decades to come as the population ages and the demands for more healthcare increase.

But healthcare is now so costly, absorbing almost 20% of the nation's GDP (gross domestic production), that it is poised to reverse course as the need to cut costs becomes paramount. As noted earlier, since labor is the largest expense, one way to cut costs is to replace labor with software and reduce the need for high-cost labor through new processes.

Since 40% of total U.S. healthcare costs are estimated to be paper-pushing—insurance claims, reviews of claims, etc.—it's blindingly obvious that streamlining the payment process could save billions of dollars. Such a streamlining is necessary, and it will reduce the number of workers processing paper in the system.

An extraordinary percentage (as high as 40%) of Medicare expenses are fraudulent, needless or counter-productive. Clearly, the system is ripe for reforms that slash needless expenses (and jobs).

Higher education is another case in point. For decades, anyone with a PhD degree could count on a job somewhere in the college/university system, as the number of those with PhDs was small and the sector was expanding. Given that the number of PhDs was limited and the demand for instructors was rising, basic supply and demand made getting a PhD a low-risk career choice.

But all that has changed. As more people flocked to the "sure thing" of earning a PhD, the number of those with advanced degrees soared. As the cost of college tuition has skyrocketed, there are now limits on the expansion of higher education. Technology is offering new methods of teaching and learning, and there is now a surplus of PhDs and master's degrees.

Soaring costs are causing a reaction that promises to slash costs and jobs in higher education. Add the surplus of qualified candidates and we have a much different supply-demand situation: no wonder so many PhDs are underemployed or unable to land a tenured spot in academia.

The inevitable reversal of trends is expressed in the phrase, "trees don't grow to the moon." This lifecycle of rapid growth, maturation and decline or collapse is a key dynamic in economics and the job market, and I use two concepts to explain it: *diminishing returns* and the *S-Curve*.

I will have more to say on those later, but for now the point is every jobseeker needs to be able to make their own assessment of which sectors are expanding and which are likely to shrink, and which ones have attracted a surplus of qualified applicants. If we understand the economy as a dynamic ecosystem where transformation, birth and death are the one constant, then we understand the importance of developing skills that can be transferred from one sector to another.

There will always be a need for nurses, dental hygienists, welders, carpenters, researchers, etc., but that doesn't mean there will automatically be jobs for everyone who is qualified to work in these fields. Supply and demand are constantly shifting, and the odds generally favor those who seek fields with a shortage of qualified applicants, or fields that are too new to have credentialing programs, where experience counts more than degrees.

Everyone seeking a livelihood has to be aware that the pace of these changes is speeding up: what looks secure now could be insecure a few years down the road. Security comes not from betting on whatever is riding high at the moment but from developing skills that are valuable in all sectors.

Even traditional fields such as law enforcement, healthcare and government are being transformed (usually when there isn't enough money to continue funding the old ways).

Understanding basic economic concepts helps us realistically assess the job market and make strategic decisions that improve our odds of success. For example, it's been found that small companies that are expanding create the most new jobs; large corporations create few new jobs, and small businesses that stay small tend to lose almost as many jobs as they create as new small business jobs are offset by those that are lost when small businesses close down.

I promised to keep the economics lesson short, and we're going to cover a lot of ground in a few pages. What I want you to understand is that capitalism and technology are both disruptive by their very nature. That mature industries shrink or disappear is not the fault of one policy or another;

that process of *creative destruction* (a term coined by economist Joseph Schumpeter) is the heart of capitalism and technology.

Many have attempted to keep technology safely locked up so it can't creatively destroy their regime or industry. But technology is a genie that cannot be kept in the bottle: *those not busy being born are busy dying.* Every nation or industry that tries to protect itself from technological transformation either stagnates or fails.

The Five Flavors of Conventional Economics

Let's start with a quick overview of the five major economic theories that dominate our era.

If you have an interest in economics, these are already familiar. If not, you've probably seen the key words in media stories. The points I want you to take home in this overview are:

1. Systems reverse or decay once extremes are reached.

2. Systems have a lifecycle of expansion, maturity and decay.

3. All economic systems are reactions to the extremes of previous systems.

For example, modern free-market capitalism arose in reaction to the limits of the feudal system and Marxism arose to explain how unrestrained capitalism leads to the dominance of finance, uncompetitive monopolies and the impoverishment of labor.

The failure of free-market capitalism (this premise is open to debate) to escape the Great Depression led to Keynesian policies of stimulus and deficit spending.

Government regulations on capital led to slow growth (again open to debate), which triggered the neoliberal capitalist agenda of loosening regulations to spur growth.

The inequalities (i.e. winners and losers) of unfettered capitalism led to state socialism, where the government reduces inequality by taxing those with high incomes and using the tax revenues to fund social programs for low-income and unemployed citizens.

In roughly the order of their emergence on the world stage:

1.	*Modern Capitalism:* this is the classical free-market capitalism: supply and demand discover price of goods, services, labor, money and risk in open, transparent markets. Business cycles are an expected feature of free-market capitalism; when credit expands, so does the economy; when credit contracts, marginal investments become insolvent and are written off; the result is recession.

2.	*Marxism:* developed by Karl Marx in the second half of 19th century, Marxist analysis holds that private capital has a built-in advantage over labor, and left to its own devices capital will impoverish laborers and enrich the owners of capital. The most profitable state of affairs for capital is not competitive free markets but the elimination of competition with monopolies or cartels.

There are multiple forms of capital (industrial, financial) but the dominant form is financial. Advanced capitalism boils down to the dominance of finance capital over industrial capital and labor. The impoverishment of labor leads to the crisis of capitalism, as eventually there aren't enough workers with sufficient income to buy the goods produced by capitalism. The Marxist critique drove the development of various flavors of socialism.

3.	*Socialist State Capitalism:* unfettered capitalism creates great disparities in income and wealth (i.e. winners and losers). The solution is to extract wealth from the free-market winners via taxes for social programs that distribute the nation's wealth more equitably. To keep private capital from dominating the economy and ruling the nation, the state owns or controls key industries.

4.	*Neo-Keynesian State Capitalism:* to counter recessions, the state (government) increases its own borrowing and spending (called deficit spending) to compensate for declining private consumption, and the central bank lowers the cost of borrowing money and floods the banking system with credit to persuade households and businesses to borrow money to spend and invest.

5.	*Neoliberal Global Capitalism:* government regulations and meddling (i.e. picking winners and losers rather than letting the free market select winners and losers) hamper growth, and without growth prosperity declines for rich and poor alike. The solution is to cut regulatory red tape and unleash markets to allow the free flow of information, labor and capital. This freedom increases the pie of wealth for everyone in the economy.

It's important to note that these systems do not necessarily replace one another; in the modern post-World War II era, each new system is layered on top of the existing arrangement. Thus state socialism didn't replace free-market capitalism; it was added as a new layer that distributed income to social programs and controlled key industries. The increased role of the state (Keynesian policies) influenced free-market capitalism but did not displace it, and neoliberal globalization extended the free flow of capital even as it left many domestic industries virtually untouched.

Entire shelves of books have been written on each of these topics, but there are five key takeaways for those seeking a career:

A. All systems generate reactions when they reach extremes/diminishing returns.

B. None of these systems is transitioning to a sustainable economy with plentiful opportunities: all are outdated and structurally flawed.

C. Every major economy is a mix of two or more of these concepts.

D. All these systems share a central faith in centralization: increasing centralization is seen as the solution to all problems.

E. Large, centralized systems are the wrong unit size for today's problems.

Let's examine these five takeaways in greater depth.

Why Systems Decline/Fail

All systems share a number of universal characteristics. Identifying these universal traits is the task of *systems analysis*. Within this enormous subject, let's focus on two dynamics mentioned above: *diminishing returns* and the *S-Curve*.

The S-curve refers to the curving line traced out by systems as they proceed through the lifecycle of introduction, expansion, maturity and decline. The nearly flat lower line of the S reflects the slow growth of the introductory stage, the rising curve reflects the phase of rapid expansion, and the flat top of the S reflects the low growth of maturity. The curve then turns down as the system declines or decays.

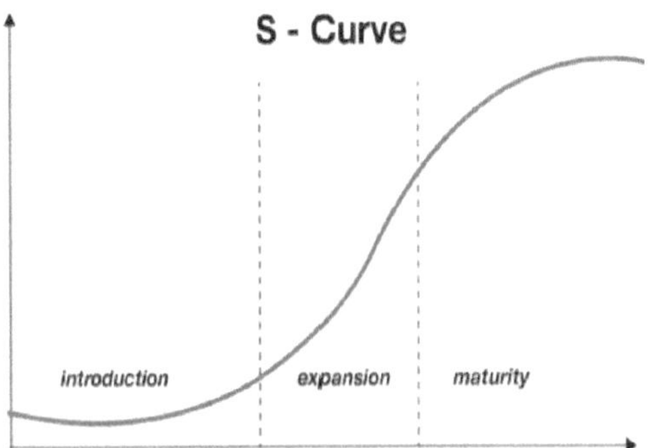

An astonishing variety of systems, both natural and human-made, conform to this lifecycle curve: infectious diseases, fashion fads and new technologies spread in a nearly identical curve, reach a phase of slowing growth and then enter a final phase of decline and collapse.

We can understand this in a number of ways, but the easiest is to understand that every system has limits, and when those limits are reached, the system runs out of steam.

For example: an infectious disease can only infect everyone without immunity to the disease. If the disease quickly kills every host it infects, it dies off with the hosts.

Every new technology can only be bought by those interested in that technology. Once everybody has one, upgrades and fashion may drive continued sales but the period of rapid expansion ends and sales stagnate.

Every system reaches saturation, and the expansion phase ends. We see this all the time in retail chains: some new franchise explodes on the scene, rapidly multiplies until it seems like there's one on every block. Eventually the market is saturated, no new stores open, and the next phase is the chain closing hundreds of underperforming stores.

I use the analogy of oxygen because we all understand that once organisms have consumed all the oxygen in a room, they expire.

In the case of college tuition and fees, these have reached the level where the majority of families cannot pay them without a loan that is as large as a home mortgage. College tuition has in effect consumed all the oxygen in the room: people can't afford to pay more, regardless of what the universities claim as expenses.

Diminishing returns refers to the way that doing more of what worked in the past eventually yields little return.

Let's say a village occupies a narrow river valley with limited flat land. To increase the yield of their farms, they start carrying water from the river up to new fields on the slopes of the valley.

At first, this additional investment of work (energy/calories and time) yields excellent returns: the amount of food grown by the village expands rapidly.

But once all the lower slopes are cultivated, the yield declines: it now takes significantly more energy and time to carry water to the higher slopes. As the farmers extend upward to the highest reaches, the amount of energy needed to carry enough water to the heights is the same amount of energy stored in the harvested crops: it makes no sense to add more farmland because the yield has diminished to zero.

One thing we've learned from behavioral economics is that humans are intellectually lazy, not because they're slothful but because the brain uses a great amount of energy. It made sense when food was scarce to stick to whatever worked in the past rather than expend a lot of calories thinking up new way of doing things.

The lower risk strategy is to stick with what works rather than gamble that a new way might work better.

As a result, when a new problem arises, we tend to substitute a solution we already know rather than work through a real solution. This is the basis of the well-known tendency for militaries to prepare for the last war rather than for wars of the future, which are difficult to anticipate and hard to plan for.

In our example, the farmers kept doing what had worked in the past until it no longer worked. But since humans tend to credit their efforts when they succeed and rationalize their failures by blaming other factors, the farmers didn't conclude their plan to keep increasing yields by farming higher slopes had failed—they blamed the weather, the gods, competing factions in the valley, etc.

This understanding that human irrationality serves a purpose in the expansion phase of the S-Curve but fails catastrophically in the decline/collapse phase is the foundation of behavioral economics.

All these economic systems have reached diminishing returns; all are failing. Yet we cling to them because we're convinced that because they made sense in the past, they will continue to make sense of the present.

It's worth noting that four of the five economic flavors are basically unchanged from the 19th century, and the fifth (Keynesian deficit spending) originated in the early 1930s. Consider how much has fundamentally changed since 1930, in demographics, technology, globalization, energy, resource depletion, etc., and then consider that all of these enormous transformations are supposed to be explained and managed by ideas that arose in a much different era.

We are programmed to keep using what has worked in the past, even when it is failing, and to blame this systemic failure on a lack of something outside our control (a limited budget, etc.).

We don't need a new technology as much as we need a new way of organizing the economy. Yet the mainstream of education, government, media, think tanks, business, unions, etc., clings to these concepts that were devised in much different eras and circumstances. We substitute problems and solutions we already know for the real problems that need new solutions.

There are no 100% ideologically pure economies—virtually every major economy is a complex mix of free markets, social program spending, Keynesian stimulus and neoliberal globalization. The U.S. , widely considered a free-market economy, devotes $2.5 trillion of its $3.8 trillion Federal budget to social programs. European nations such as Germany that are considered social-democratic rely heavily on globalization and exports to fund their social spending. China, nominally Communist, relies on free markets to generate the revenues needed to subsidize state-owned enterprises (SOEs).

The point I want you to take away from this is that we don't have *one economy; we have a multitude of economies mixed together*. These economies co-exist, and can be imagined as layers that overlap each other in certain areas but operate by their own rules and inputs.

For example, those with jobs in state social programs are working in a quite different environment than those exposed to free market forces. Those working in globalized sectors have a much different set of conditions than those working in domestically protected sectors such as law enforcement.

As all the protected sectors enter diminishing returns, pressures to modernize and cut costs are inevitable.

It is essential to understand the economy's multiple layers, because each one operates on a different wavelength and requires a different set of career strategies.

I hope you now understand why those sectors *that aren't busy being born are busy dying*: any system that isn't constantly adapting will inevitably reach diminishing returns and the point of decline/collapse on the S-Curve. This is true of enterprises, systems and entire economies.

Though these economic flavors are quite different, they share one characteristic that has itself reached diminishing returns: centralization.

Though free market economies allow for a wide spectrum of businesses, modern capitalism is dominated by cartel-state capitalism: most of the power, capital and control have been aggregated into centralized cartels and the government.

I illustrate this by asking a simple question: where does 90% of your household income go? Home mortgages are a major expense: most mortgages are held by one of five banks and insured by a government housing agency. When a handful of companies dominate a sector, it's a cartel. When one company is the only choice available, it's a monopoly. In most areas, there are only two providers of health insurance; there are often only one or two providers of broadband Internet service. The same is true of mobile phone services. Fast food is dominated by a handful of national chains, as are grocery stores.

If you add up where your household income goes, in most cases you will find the vast majority goes to centralized organizations: government (taxes) and large corporations that claim to be competitive but which are actually cartels or quasi-monopolies. Most of the money in our economy flows to centralized organizations.

During the long process of industrialization, the *economies of scale* mentioned earlier gave centralized organizations significant advantages over small competitors. When government encountered a problem, the solution is always a new centralized agency to oversee and enforce new regulations. Whatever the problem, the solution has always been more centralization.

It is a central thesis of this book that centralization has reached diminishing returns and is no longer yielding any benefit. Instead, it has become the problem, not the solution; what worked in the past no longer works now. Centralization as a solution has been leapfrogged by decentralizing technologies.

The World Wide Web enables decentralized networks of productivity and cooperation that operate without centralized authority. The most productive and lowest-cost system turns out to be decentralized, not a centralized arrangement where capital and political power are concentrated into the hands of a few at the top of the heap.

Complex systems eventually reach a point on the S-Curve where they cannot be effectively managed by a top-down hierarchy, regardless of the competence or intelligence of the managers.

Here's the final takeaway: these economic systems are failing because they're the *wrong unit size*: Large, centralized systems are incapable of providing solutions for today's problems, which as noted above are changing demographics, resource depletion, rising costs of energy, changing nature of work (i.e. the end of work) and social recession. These are not ideological problems, so ideologies cannot provide answers.

If solutions must be decentralized and distributed, then bureaucratic centralized organizations cannot possibly be a solution: they're the wrong unit size.

Since we are hardwired to grab a solution we know for every new problem rather than look for new solutions, it's to be expected that the vast majority of people are reaching for a solution they already know—one of these 19th century ideologies—rather than face the reality that these are no longer solutions, they are the problem.

How does this help everyone seeking a livelihood?

It boils down to this: Don't set your sights on entering the buggy-whip industry. And if you do, understand at the start that the competition for the dwindling number of jobs will be fierce and the security of the industry is diminishing every day because it's no longer a solution.

The systems that survive and prosper are those that are exposed to dynamics that force constant evolution, adaptation and innovation, i.e. coming up with new solutions rather than just grabbing an old one and hoping it solves the new problem.

Those people who are also evolving, adapting and experimenting with new solutions to new problems will always be in demand.

So the takeaway from our brief examination of economic flavors and systems is simple: seek sectors and organizations that are adapting and seeking real solutions, and try to become a person who does the same, regardless of what field you're working in.

The Five Types of Capitalism

Capitalism is bandied about as if it was one system, but free-market capitalism isn't monolithic: there are five basic types of capitalism, and once again those seeking a livelihood will push the odds in their favor by understanding that not all types of capitalism offer the same opportunities.

Broadly speaking, capitalism is an economic and social system based on private ownership and transparent markets for the exchange and distribution of goods and services. While these attributes of capitalism can be traced back to early trading communities, the modern version of capitalism depends on transparent markets not just for goods and services but also for capital, labor, risk and credit.

Transparent markets discover the price of goods, services, labor, capital, risk and credit, and as a result they provide discipline that discourages high-risk, low-return speculative bets, inefficiency and waste.

The core of capitalism is of course *capital*: capital that is invested to earn a profit, i.e. accumulate more capital. Capital is generally assumed to mean money, but non-financial capital is just as important as financial capital in a knowledge-based economy such as ours. This is why we will examine the five types of non-financial capital in depth later in this section.

Some attributes of capitalism can be viewed as expressions of human nature rather than ideological constructs. The pursuit of self-interest drives competition and what Adam Smith called *the invisible hand* of the market. It is also the reason that capital seeks the highest return.

Self-interest all too easily veers into greed and avarice, and as a result all economic systems have the potential to exploit shared resources (i.e. the commons) and other people. This is a feature not just of capitalism but of all social and political orders. The Elites in feudal societies, monarchies, theocracies and socialist systems all manage the status quo to enrich themselves and preserve their power.

In my book *Resistance, Revolution, Liberation: A Model for Positive Change,* I outline the following five basic types of capitalism (though variations of these are equally visible in monarchies, theocracies and socialism):

1. Extractive
2. Exploitative
3. Enterprise
4. Marketing
5. Corporate/State

Extractive capitalism is based on the gain reaped by the extraction of an asset in the environment, such as a metals mine or fishery. Once the resource is depleted, capital moves on, seeking another high-yielding investment. (The fact that the environment is ruined doesn't count, as capitalism has no way to value the commons or estimate future costs resulting from extracting resources.)

Exploitative capitalism is based on the monopolistic control of labor and other productive assets such as land. A classic example is a plantation with indentured labor.

Enterprise capitalism rewards capital invested when the leverage of innovation and competitive advantage is greatest, and heaps the greatest gains on innovations in technology and other means of production.

Marketing capitalism is based on the stimulation of previously non-existent (and generally superfluous) wants and impulses. This generates, and profits from, the consumerist ideology—you can never have enough of anything. Marketing capitalism requires ubiquitous access to credit as the fuel for instant gratification.

Corporate/State capitalism is the institutionalization of cartel capitalism in partnership with the State: the State enables and protects quasi-monopolies to fund its own agencies/fiefdoms.

A cartel is an organization of nominally competing enterprises that fixes prices and production to benefit its members. Cartels may be formal, such as the Organization of Oil Exporting Nations (OPEC) or informal. Informal cartels often rely on government regulations to restrict competitors' entry into their market and to enforce an *artificial scarcity* of the cartel's products or services. To mask the uncompetitive nature of their cartel, members devote enormous resources to public relations.

Examples include the healthcare system and higher education, both of which are informal cartels.

Why This Matters to Jobseekers

What does this matter to those seeking a livelihood? Once again, the answer is the high likelihood of systemic responses to diminishing returns. Let's take each type of capitalism and consider the likely impact of systemic responses on career opportunities.

Extractive industries: the world can ill-afford the *external costs* of extractive capitalism—the despoiled landscapes left by certain types of mining, the desert-like emptiness of oceans stripped of fish, and so on. The inability to price the external costs of habitat destruction, loss of diversity, restoration of drained wetlands and polluted watersheds, etc., is a core failing of free-market capitalism, which only discovers the price of goods and services via current supply and demand.

Clearly, wildlife habitat management is necessary to restore ravaged natural systems. Advances in mining that do not destroy the environment are needed. The market for sustainable aquaculture can only expand as alternatives to wild fisheries become the lowest-impact source of shellfish and fish. (Note the emphasis on sustainable—not all aquaculture is sustainable or low-impact.)

In other words, the response to the extremes of despoliation will create jobs in more sustainable, lower-impact alternatives to current practices.

Exploitative capitalism: exploitative capitalism thrives in captive labor markets with few opportunities for entrepreneurship and advancement. The ideal situation for exploitative capital is a poorly educated populace under the thumb of Elites who offer few opportunities for starting a business or earning money. A factory can be set up and workers hired for extremely low wages because labor is abundant and cash work is scarce.

Web-based technologies for low-cost education (such as $40 tablets preloaded with software that teaches children to read and write) and peer-to-peer lending and marketing all greatly expand opportunities outside the control of rapacious Elites. These are positive opportunities in economies vulnerable to exploitative capitalism.

Enterprise capitalism: as noted earlier, large global companies create relatively few jobs. Opportunities are higher in enterprises that adapt quickly and *establish systems to consistently experiment* with new ideas and drop those that don't pan out. The extremes of centralized capital are drawing a systemic reaction: peer-to-peer networks are bypassing corporations and small businesses are expanding in markets that are too small to attract centralized capital.

Marketing capitalism: given the stagnation of the bottom 90% of household incomes and the rise in household debt (including student loans), it is impossible for debt-based consumerism to expand in the bottom 90% of the economy.

This leaves those seeking a career in marketing-stimulated capitalism two choices: either concentrate on the top 10% segment of households that still have disposable income—a segment that is already crowded with competitors —or seek opportunities in the Degrowth/decentralization movements that seek to do more with less by abandoning superfluous consumption.

Corporate/State capitalism: the private-sector/state regulated cartels that dominate defense, healthcare, etc., are beset by diminishing returns: weapons systems such as the F-35 Lightning are unaffordable and offer minimal advances over previous systems that cost a mere 20% of the F-35 program, U.S. healthcare now consumes 20% of the economy, double the per capita costs of other advanced economies, and higher education is unaffordable to the bottom 90% without government loans that turn every student into a debt-serf.

Student-loan debt-serfdom is what I term *neofeudalism,* that is, an updated version of feudalism in which debt that cannot be discharged in bankruptcy has become the new means of enforcing servitude.

Since these state-managed cartels are considered secure employers, the competition for careers within them is increasing, even as the inevitable reaction to their diminishing returns is gathering strength.

Opportunities will be expanding in defense enterprises that cut the cost of weaponry by 50%, not those that increase costs four-fold. These will likely be new, small enterprises, not global corporations. Opportunities in adaptive learning and other aspects of new educational strategies covered in my book *The Nearly Free University* will expand as the bloated and unaffordable higher education cartel sheds jobs.

Government itself will be revolutionized as existing state systems go bankrupt due to unrealistic promises, declining Degrowth-era tax revenues and diminishing returns on centralized bureaucracies. Opportunities will expand for those offering government new ways of providing services at a fraction of the cost of current systems.

Healthcare can no longer consume more money every year; it has already consumed all the available oxygen. Opportunities will expand in preventive medicine, cash-only clinics and systems that radically streamline overhead and the costs of delivering healthcare at home rather than in high-cost centralized hospitals.

The point here is that extremes of exploitation, extraction, inefficiency, cronyism and diminishing returns all inevitably spark a systemic response. Opportunity lies not in bloated bureaucracies or marketing debt-based consumption but in the systemic responses that are powered by the need for sustainable, non-debt alternatives.

What I term *the emerging economy* is not a separate type of capitalism; it is the result of *digital-software-fabrication-robotics-automation (DSFRA)* technologies sweeping through the five types of capitalism in an uneven but inevitable reconfiguration of the current arrangement.

Though the media tends to focus on the technology sector as the source of innovation, every sector of capitalism is being transformed as the DSFRA technologies enable alternatives that dramatically lower costs and expand opportunities for those outside centralized bureaucracies. Centralized organizations will have to decentralize to get closer to customers and clients (including taxpayers) and cut costs, and they will have to shed expenses—the most expensive one being labor.

As we saw with the various economic systems, new technologies revolutionize processes in existing sectors and add new layers of enterprise rather than replace old ones. Some industries and jobs are obsoleted out of existence in this process—buggy whips and lamplighters, for example—but the takeaway for jobseekers is to look for opportunity not just in new fields but in established sectors that are being transformed by DSFRA technologies.

It is critically important to understand the more hidebound and old-fashioned the industry, the greater the gains to be reaped by introducing DSFRA technologies.

In most cases, an enormous number of jobs are wiped out when technology transforms a sector. Consider agriculture as an example: in the 19th century, roughly 50% of the workforce toiled on farms. Now roughly 2%

of the workforce works in agriculture. At the turn of the 20th century, the largest job category was domestic help.

But if we widen our understanding of the economy beyond the dominant state-cartel model of capitalism, we will find expansive opportunities in the emergent free-market *community economy*. (I will describe the community economy in more detail later.)

The more those seeking a career understand how free-market capitalism works, the more the odds shift in their favor. Opportunity is not randomly distributed; it gathers where the conditions favor it. To find the best opportunities, we need to understand the key dynamics of free-market capitalism. Remember: *your advantage is knowledge.*

Each Layer of the Economy Operates on a Different Wavelength

Each layer of the economy operates on a different wavelength: the rules, contexts and ways of doing things are different in each one. It's important for jobseekers to understand the norms of the layer they want to work in.

Those seeking employment in the technocratic professional layer—the primary home of the top 10% of earners—have to navigate a much different environment than those working in small enterprises, technology and industrial production. We will cover this in more depth later, but the takeaway here is that the economy is not monolithic: it is a constantly changing swirl of established industries being transformed by technology, sectors resisting this transformation, emerging industries, fields still dominated by insider-spoils systems and *do-ocracies* where those who do the most gain the most influence and earnings.

The odds favor those who understand the norms of the layer they want to work in.

Mobile Capital and Creative Destruction

One aspect of capitalism that disturbs many people is the mobile nature of capital—that capital will flow to the highest return, regardless of national borders or religious, national and ideological loyalties.

Capital that doesn't seek to expand will fall victim to capitalism's process of natural selection, what economist Joseph Schumpeter termed *creative destruction*: the only way innovation and productive investment can occur is if less productive investments and quasi-monopolies are dismantled. As a result, corporations and those tasked with managing capital become (using Peter Drucker's invocation of an old Soviet phrase) *rootless cosmopolitans*, moving financial and human capital where they will earn the highest return. The same can be said of mobile workers, who move in order to find better-paying work or advance their career.

Just as financial capital must grow or face creative destruction, *human capital*—skills and knowledge—must also be constantly reworked to align with changing market and social forces. To decry this is to decry the reality that the world is constantly changing and we must adapt or suffer the consequences.

From the long-term perspective of human development, extracting a living from Nature is inherently insecure. Hunter-gatherers have to constantly locate new (or renewed) sources of food and water, and agriculture without irrigation is exposed to the risks of drought, flood, insect infestations, etc. Traditional societies were thus geared toward conserving social systems that organized labor, authority, grain distribution, etc. in ways that reduced such insecurity. This desire for security favored traditional means of enforcing stability, but also discouraged risk and innovation.

Capitalist enterprises are organized solely to seek profit and expand capital, and as a result they disrupt these established risk-averse social and economic arrangements. Since capitalism thrives on risk-taking, innovation, mobile capital and the free exchange of ideas, goods and services, it rewards disruptive improvements in productivity. As a result, capitalism soon outpaces traditional methods.

Everything from the structure of families to the political order is disrupted by rapid changes in production and distribution of goods and services. As a result, there is always a tension between capitalism and the traditionally conservative social and political order.

It is important to understand the democratizing power of modern capitalism's financial system. The core features of modern finance—joint stock companies, stock exchanges and risk-management hedges—were present in European hotbeds of capitalism by the 1400s. Capitalism's ability to raise capital from diverse sources and lend it to a variety of enterprises enabled a new class—entrepreneurs—to arise. From that point on, enterprise was not limited to the aristocracy; people outside the small circle of the feudal Elite suddenly had access to capital.

Capitalism developed as a *self-organizing* way to share and price risk, and to spread losses from failed ventures and loans. By enabling small investors to pool capital, the system created a broad-based mechanism for distributing both profits and losses.

In a continuation of this dynamic, today the Internet is enabling crowdsourced sources of credit such as micro-loans. Credit is escaping from the tyranny of the big banks and their partners, the central bank and state.

In our highly politicized society, it's become habit to render the world black or white, Left or Right, Conservative or Progressive, etc.: every trend is declared good or bad. Free-market capitalism (as opposed to the state-cartel version that dominates our economy) is neither good nor bad; it is simply a system that favors adaptation over conserving the traditional ways. Its innate drive to democratize capital is inherently progressive, and this is why state-cartel capitalism (also called crony capitalism) seeks to eliminate competition and transparency, the two essentials of free-market capitalism.

What makes free-market capitalism easy to love or hate is that it disrupts social and economic arrangements without regard to borders, politics or our own likes and dislikes. Those who see it disrupting oppressive social and economic arrangements view it as liberating, while those whose security depended on inefficient, corrupt, obsolete systems maintaining power indefinitely view it as destructive.

Free-market capitalism is akin to natural selection in Nature: it operates not on likes and dislikes or to protect those currently atop the heap but on what adaptations work best in a changing environment.

Free-Market Capitalism Breaks Down Barriers, State-Cartel Capitalism Erects Them

The core dynamic of capitalism in our era is the battle between free-market capitalism, which breaks down barriers that protect the status quo's profits, and state-cartel capitalism which erects barriers that keep out competitors and guarantee high costs and fat profits. Barriers protect entrenched elites.

One example is print media's former lock hold on classified advertisements. Before Craigslist and other free classified advertising websites, anyone wanting to sell something had to pay a newspaper to print a classified ad. The tiny ads were expensive, and classified ad income was a stable revenue foundation for newspapers.

The Internet tore down that barrier, lowering costs to near-zero and destroying the classified-ad barrier.

In contrast, state-regulated cartels erect barriers that increase their profits by eliminating competition or raising the cost of doing business so high that no new enterprise can afford to enter the sector.

Another barrier is erected by enforcing *artificial scarcity*: now that education is digital, there is no technical reason why someone could not take college courses online, pass the exams online and be issued a diploma online, all for virtually free. The higher education cartel protects its vast income from college tuition by artificially restricting college diplomas.

A thicket of complicated regulations also acts as a barrier to new competition, as few firms can muster the legal expertise to navigate thousands of pages of state regulations. I call this barrier a *complexity fortress*, as the complexity of the regulations act as a fortress, protecting the profits of the cartel.

Healthcare is a prime example of a complexity fortress, as the Affordable Care Act's thousands of pages of regulations eliminate smaller companies from competing.

Free-market capitalism tends to go around barriers with new technologies and social innovations. Free-market capitalism enables fast evolution and low-cost experimentation, a dynamic expressed by the phrase, "fail fast, fail often."

Consider the cost of renting a hotel room when traveling. Government regulations define a hotel in such a way that only extremely wealthy individuals and corporations could possibly own or start a hotel.

Peer-to-peer services such as AirBnB bypassed this capital-intensive, highly regulated model of providing rooms to visitors by making any spare bedroom in a home or flat into an alternative hotel room. This system is opt-in, meaning anyone who wants to offer a room can do so, and anyone seeking a room can rent the room if they choose to do so. There is no centralized bureaucracy managing the options or choices.

The state-cartel economy is characterized by middlemen (distributors) that add layers of cost, while free-market capitalism seeks to cut out middlemen and enable sales directly from producers to end users. This is the basic strength of farmers' markets and farm-to-consumer networks.

Information asymmetry is another type of barrier. U.S. healthcare erects barriers by withholding the price of services and obscuring the true costs of care, making it impossible for end users to make informed decisions based on competitive apples-to-apples comparisons of quality and price.

The state enforces barriers that protect cartels and professional guilds, always under the banner of protecting consumers. But beneath this public-service veneer, the agenda pushed by lobbyists is protecting status quo costs and profits.

Barriers are *self-liquidating*, meaning that the negative consequences of barriers—inefficiency, high costs, stagnation—eventually erode the barriers. At some point, people can no longer afford the high prices created by barriers, and a black market or *informal economy* arises to provide the goods and services which have become too expensive in the formal barrier-protected economy.

When middlemen and regulations add value, the value is noticeable to the end consumer. When they cease adding value and simply add cost (i.e. when barriers to competition have been erected), consumers abandon the protected sector and seek alternatives.

Free-market capitalism excels in developing alternatives that bypass or dismantle barriers, lowering costs, broadening choices, inviting competition and improving quality. State-cartel capitalism excels in erecting barriers to protect politically powerful guilds and cartels.

We can characterize the two as different approaches to security: state-cartel capitalism seeks security by suppressing competition and guaranteeing high prices and profits with centralized authority, while free-market capitalism seeks security with innovation, lower costs, transparency, voluntary choices and decentralized local control.

State-cartel capitalism seeks security with "too big to fail," while free-market capitalism seeks security with "fail fast, fail often, and stay close to customers and local markets."

Which system is guaranteed to fail? The one that is too big to fail, as too big to fail means it is too big to be managed effectively in a centralized fashion.

Barriers enable people to get complacent. Those protected by barriers lose sight of the organization's purpose and ignore the symptoms as the organization slides into the decline/collapse phase of the S-Curve.

Which is better, creative destruction by superior methods, or the stagnation and high costs of protected cartels? In either case, the result is still the same: barriers are self-liquidating.

The Essential Role of Credit, Property Rights and Rule of Law

Property rights, rule of law and credit all have key roles in capitalism. Credit-starved economies with limited private ownership rights are underdeveloped economies, as economist Hernando De Soto explained in his book, *The Mystery of Capital: Why Capitalism Triumphs in the West and Fails Everywhere Else.* In the chronically underdeveloped economies De Soto describes, households have assets—land, dwellings, small businesses—but since the assets do not have legal status as "property" (because the system for recognizing and registering property is cumbersome and/or corrupt), the assets cannot act as collateral for borrowed capital (i.e. loans).

A state that can be corrupted to protect entrenched Elites at the expense of private property is a state where free markets and democracy are stunted – and as a result, so too are opportunity and prosperity.

Credit plays a key role in capitalism's success and also its failure. When credit is unavailable to entrepreneurs, innovations go begging and the economy stagnates under entrenched Elites. Conversely, when credit is so cheap and plentiful that unproductive projects are funded, the eventual collapse of these malinvestments brings down the entire financial system. (This is what happened in 2008.)

Colonial America provides an example of a credit-starved economy. In the wake of the Revolutionary war and the ratification of the Constitution (1789), the U.S. financial system was a mess: debts left by the war burdened the new government, which historian Thomas McCaw noted "started on a shoestring and almost immediately went bankrupt."

Ordinary farmers and entrepreneurs were desperate for long-term credit to fuel their rapidly growing enterprises. Though states were banned by the Constitution from issuing their own currency, states got around this prohibition by granting bank charters. The banks promptly issued the credit that an entrepreneurial economy needed. The political Elite, regardless of their differences, were appalled by this explosion of privately issued and largely unregulated credit, but this access to credit fueled the astonishing growth of the U.S. economy in the 1790's and early 1800's.

The nascent American economy in this phase was anything but orderly or well-regulated. The terms "wild" and "risky" better describe the financial and commercial chaos of the era, but this untamed capitalism led to more successes than failures. The chaotic explosion of credit and entrepreneurial drive was the opposite of central planning, be it Communist, theocratic or nominally capitalist. Risk was everywhere; security according to today's meaning did not exist.

Risk cannot be eliminated; it can only be suppressed or transferred to others. This is the lesson of mathematician Benoit Mandelbrot's book, *The Misbehavior of Markets: A Fractal View of Financial Turbulence.* Though government social welfare programs have eased the insecurity that comes with constant innovation and disruption, there is no way to eliminate risk from free markets, or indeed, from life itself.

Cooperation, Innovation and Risk Management

One feature of capitalism that is rarely noted is the premium placed on cooperation. The Darwinian aspect of competition is widely accepted (and rued) as capitalism's dominant force, but cooperation is just as intrinsic to capitalism as competition. Subcontractors must cooperate to assemble a product, suppliers must cooperate to deliver the various components, distributors must cooperate to get the products to retail outlets, employees and managers must cooperate to reach the goals of the organization, and local governments and communities must cooperate with enterprises to maintain the local economy.

Darwin's understanding of natural selection is often misapplied. In its basic form, natural selection simply means that the world is constantly changing, and organisms must adapt or they will expire. The same is true of individuals, enterprises, governments, cultures and economies. Darwin wrote: *"It is not the strongest of the species that survives, or the most intelligent, but the ones most adaptable to change."*

Ideas, techniques and processes which are better and more productive than previous versions will spread quickly; those who refuse to adapt them will be overtaken by those who do. These new ideas, techniques and processes trigger changes in society and the economy that are often difficult to predict.

This creates a dilemma: we want more prosperity and wider opportunities for self-cultivation (personal fulfillment), yet we don't want our security and culture to be disrupted. But we cannot have it both ways. Those who attempt to preserve their power over the social order while reaping the gains of free markets find their power dissolving before their eyes as unintended consequences of technological and social innovations disrupt their mechanisms of control.

Yet rejecting free markets also fails to preserve the power structure, for a citizenry denied the opportunity to prosper chafes under a Status Quo that enriches Elites and relegates the masses to stagnation and poverty.

The great irony of free-market capitalism is that the only way to establish an enduring security is to embrace innovation and adaptation, the very processes that generate short-term insecurity. Attempting to guarantee security leads to risk being distributed to others, or concentrated within the system itself. When the accumulated risk manifests, the system collapses.

The core dynamic of free markets is the causal links between the free movement of labor and capital, transparent markets, risk, adaptation and growth. Every attempt to eliminate risk, hinder the flow of capital, rig markets and limit disruptive adaptation leads to stagnation and eventual collapse as the inefficient, wasteful and corrupt elements of the economy absorb all the oxygen, starving the system of investment, innovation, accountability and initiative.

We can follow Darwin's observation that *"It is not the strongest of the species that survives, or the most intelligent, but the ones most adaptable to change,"* with a corollary: *Eliminating risk eliminates the possibility of successful adaptation.*

We can go even further and suggest *adaptive advantages are correlated to risk: the lower the risk, the lower the odds of loss and the lower the advantages gained.*

Adaptation is thus a dynamic series of trade-offs between making many low-risk experiments that yield marginal losses and gains and occasional high-risk experiments that raise the stakes but which may yield game-changing advantages.

There are lessons here for jobseekers: playing it safe limits potential losses but it also limits potential gains. When an opportunity arises that requires higher risk, the risk sets up the possibility of big gains. We don't want to blindly take one big risk after another; that's a sure way to lose. The odds are best when the opportunity is low-risk and the potential gain is game-changing.

Our competitive advantage is being able to identify opportunities with the best chances of succeeding, and that requires understanding the *infrastructure of opportunity*.

The Infrastructure of Opportunity

Why do these characteristics of free-market capitalism matter to jobseekers? Opportunity is not randomly distributed; it results from what I call the *infrastructure of opportunity*. If there is no mobility of labor and capital, no transparent markets for labor and capital, no creative destruction of corrupt, obsolete, inefficient systems, weak rule of law, weak property rights, no self-organizing (i.e. not centralized) access to credit, limited means of cooperation, little room for innovation and no understanding of the essential role of risk in adaptation, opportunities are innately scarce. Virtually all bets made in this environment will be lost because there is no fertile ground—it's a desert for opportunity.

Conversely, when there are transparent markets for labor, capital and credit, plenty of mobile labor and capital, abundant ways to cooperate with others, constant creative destruction of cartels, inefficient processes and corrupt cronyism, strong rule of law and property rights and a strong appetite for innovation and risk, opportunities are abundant.

This is one reason why cities offer so many more opportunities than rural areas: cities offer more access to credit, means of cooperating, mobility of labor and capital, more opportunities for innovation to take root, and so on.

This is why those regions and nations that offer the most robust *infrastructures of opportunity* have the most dynamic economies.

Those seeking opportunities for jobs and careers have to start by moving out of the desert and into fertile territory where the *infrastructure of opportunity* enables adaptation.

The Key Takeaways

The essence of non-exploitive capitalism is *creative destruction* of current systems as more productive/profitable ways become available and barriers protecting the status quo are torn down or bypassed. As a result, capitalism inevitably disrupts current economic and social arrangements.

The decades of stable employment that characterized the post-World War II era, long considered the birthright of every resident of advanced economies, were actually anomalies made possible by low-cost resources and rapidly expanding credit. Now that resources are no longer cheap and abundant, and credit has entered diminishing returns, the inherently disruptive nature of capitalism is transforming outmoded, obsolete, inefficient and diminishing-return systems and organizations.

We are entering an extended era of disruption comparable to the industrial revolution, an era in which stability comes not from working for one employer for 30 years but from owning skills, *social capital* and *the means of production*—terms we will explore in greater depth in following chapters.

In this era, security comes from embracing adaptation and learning, rather than trying to get hired by a centralized bureaucracy for life. This emerging era will favor *do-ocracies*, where the more a person does, the more influence they will have, as opposed to bureaucracies, which seek to eliminate individual risk and accountability.

As individuals, we must adapt to this era by accepting that security comes not from clinging to obsolete arrangements that are no longer sustainable but by becoming adaptable ourselves. Capitalism and Nature both favor the most adaptable, and the opportunities will be greatest in those sectors that are most hidebound, where the gains to be reaped by transformation are the greatest.

Section Two: The Changing Nature of Work

It's not just the types of work that are changing—the nature of work itself is changing, too. The relationship between capital and labor, divided by a sharp line in the 19th century, has become much more complex in a *knowledge-based economy*--an economy whose growth depends largely on knowledge and the collaborative exchange of information.

In the industrial age of the 19th and 20th centuries, capital referred to large holdings of productive land (for example, plantations), large sums of cash that could be used to buy assets, or ownership of capital-intensive assets such as factories, mines, pipelines, electrical generation plants, etc. Assets that generate products or services are known as the *means of production*.

Ownership of large-scale capital and the means of production were reserved for financiers, industrialists and the state.

Labor had one commodity to trade or sell: time. Since labor on farms, factory floors, etc., was largely interchangeable—there was little specialization and only limited roles for expertise—labor was itself a commodity much like the grain or manufactured items the workers produced. One hour of labor bought from laborer A was little different from the hour of labor bought from Laborer B.

The key here is the process of *commodification*: when goods or services can be traded interchangeably in large quantities within free markets, these are commodities, as opposed to one-of-a-kind goods and services unique to one small-scale producer.

To a factory owner in 1910, the differences in skills within a group of 100 laborers made little difference (with the exception of highly skilled craftsmen such as tool and die makers): the assembly line moved at the same rate regardless of which individuals were on a particular shift.

Even skilled labor can be commoditized: when we hear "the doctor will see you now," what's being delivered is a defined expertise from a highly trained but nonetheless interchangeable worker.

Anything that is produced in bulk and that is interchangeable is a commodity. Though variations exist in commodities, they are still interchangeable and readily traded in markets.

What cannot be commoditized? A home-cooked family meal cannot be commoditized. A meal can be packaged in a factory and shipped to a market where the family can buy the meal, but this is not the same as a home-cooked family meal. Preparing and sharing a home-cooked meal is a shared, communal process; microwaving a package is not. The two are not interchangeable.

Money is a commodity and is interchangeable (so is credit).

One-of-a-kind objects that cannot be produced in bulk are not interchangeable and are not commodities. Examples include fine art (hence the value of passing forgeries off as the real thing), rare gemstones and items of historical significance. Goods that cannot be commoditized command high prices precisely because they are not being made in quantity and are not interchangeable.

Individuals with unique sets of difficult-to-define skills are not open to commoditization because they are not interchangeable and cannot be produced or trained in great numbers. Suppose that a biotechnology company had a new treatment for a brain disorder that it wanted patented. The ideal candidate would be an M.D. trained in brain science who was also a patent attorney. These two disciplines could be divided, but to some degree the person writing the patent would be hobbled by a lack of deep understanding of brain science. While there may be a small number of qualified candidates, there will not be many due to the many years of training required to master two quite different specialties.

Here's another example. Suppose a company that manufactures specialty metal assemblies uses welding robots to fabricate large orders of interchangeable parts. The company lands a contract for assemblies that cannot be reduced to a set series of welds; a human welder can do many but not all the welds faster and cheaper than the robot, which must be reprogrammed.

The ideal candidate is both an experienced welder and an experienced operator of the welding robot. This worker is not interchangeable with a welder or a robot operator.

Note the difference between interchangeable commodity labor and labor that is not interchangeable. What cannot be commoditized will command a higher value.

One of the basic trends of free-market capitalism is that increased specialization leads to more prosperity for everyone in the economy. The specialized worker produces more than the worker with generalized skills, and this increased production eventually lowers the cost of the product as the supply expands. The specialized worker makes more money because he produces more, and so it's win-win: products decline in price even though everyone with specialized skills is earning more money.

This is the basic argument for globalization: if one region or nation specializes in producing X, and another specializes in producing Y, trade between the two will enrich both because each can buy the product of the other for a lower price while commanding a higher price for its own products.

But specialization does not necessarily mean the labor cannot be commoditized. Since any work whose processed and point of completion can be specified can be traded or automated, specialized tasks that are *process-based work* (i.e. the processes can be specified) can still be commoditized.

Specialization is only a defense against work being automated or offshored if it is not *process-based work* and cannot be commoditized.

The only type of work that cannot be commoditized is work involving processes that cannot be specified in advance and whose point of completion is unknown. Creative work is one example. It's difficult to specify each step of an advertising campaign, for example, because the campaign is a dynamic process that is changing constantly in response to what seems to be working and what new ideas come to the team. Even the point of completion is difficult to specify: what makes the campaign a success?

If corporations could buy software for $100 that churned out advertising campaigns that worked with tremendous predictability, there would be no need for advertising agencies that charge tens of thousands of dollars.

This highlights a critical distinction between *process-based work* and work that is not reducible to a process. If a task has a defined point of completion and can be broken down into a series of steps that can be specified, it can be programmed. Once it can be programmed, it can be automated.

If the task can be broken down into simple-to-learn steps, it can be commoditized and performed anywhere in the world: the people on assembly lines are interchangeable.

The world economy has been globalized for hundreds of years (trade in silk and other precious goods date back thousands of years). Sugar, tobacco and tea were enormously profitable commodities that were shipped in great quantities thousands of miles by sea.

Advances in telecommunications and the Internet have expanded global trade from goods to services: technical support calls, for example, can be handled by someone in a distant country.

Economist Michael Spence divided goods and services into two basic categories: those that can be traded globally, i.e. imported or exported, and those that cannot be traded. Work that can be outsourced to employees overseas is a tradable service. Work that cannot be traded includes services that are localized, for example, repairing a porch railing.

Process-based work is generally tradable because the labor is commoditized; the people who complete the task are interchangeable. Work that cannot be specified is less tradable because the people who perform the work are not interchangeable.

In the previous era of globalization, the goods being traded were produced elsewhere because they could not be produced in the home market. Sugar cane, for example, does not grow well in England, so sugar was produced elsewhere and shipped to England.

What differentiates the present era of globalization is the trading of services such as tech support and software programming. This means that workers are competing with everyone else in the global village for work that is tradable. In this networked world, specialization is no longer a competitive advantage; the competitive advantage goes to those whose work cannot be commoditized or traded.

What is driving this commoditization of labor? The same force that drives the commoditization of goods and services: competition. Now that many services are also tradable, the marketplace for these services is global. Since most of the workforce in advanced economies is employed in the service sector (as opposed to agriculture, mining, energy, construction and manufacturing), the commoditization and tradability of service labor is having an enormous impact on the delivery of services and on service labor.

It's important to understand that labor is the primary cost in the service sectors. As robots have replaced humans on factory assembly lines, the labor component of manufactured goods has declined. If you want to reduce the cost of a manufactured item, reduce the number of parts by 50% and/or the amount of material by 50%. If you want to reduce the cost of a service by 50%, you reduce the labor by 50%.

As Peter Drucker observed, enterprises don't have profits, they only have expenses. The only way to maintain a competitive advantage in the global market is to reduce expenses, by trimming either the cost of production, fixed costs (office rent, etc.), or overhead costs: benefits, management, etc.

It's also important to note that the overhead costs of labor have risen dramatically in the past 20 years, and this trend shows no sign of reversing. The total cost of an employee is not just the wage/salary compensation; it includes all the labor-related overhead expenses: workers compensation insurance, disability insurance, the employer's share of Social Security and Medicare taxes, unemployment insurance, pension contributions, vacation pay and healthcare (assuming the employer pays some or all of the employee's healthcare insurance costs). Depending on the locale, industry and the age of the employee, these overhead expenses can nearly equal the wage/salary. In other words, if the employee's wage is $2,000 a month, the total compensation costs to the employer might be $4,000 a month.

Given the steady rise in healthcare and other overhead expenses, the employee may be wondering why he hasn't received a raise in years, while the employer is looking at the rising costs of benefits and total compensation costs. The employee might be costing the employer an additional $500 a month but all of this money is invisible to the employee, as it goes not to him but to healthcare insurance premiums.

This is why it's necessary for the nation to lower the costs of state-cartel systems like healthcare; as these price-insensitive, politically protected systems continue to increase their share of the national income, there's less money available for wages outside the cartel.

In other words, the pressure on wages has little to do with any one employer or sector; it results from systemic distortions in the economy and global competition that cannot be put back in the bottle.

Machines have a built-in cost advantage over human employees, simply because they do not incur labor overhead costs: they do not get sick, do not need vacations, do not go on strike, and their costs of maintenance are more predictable than the costs of healthcare for human employees.

All these factors push employers to reduce labor costs by commoditizing work so it can be automated or performed by cheaper labor overseas.

Though much work has been commoditized, and much more can be commoditized, a significant amount of work cannot be automated or performed overseas; this includes everything from lining domestic oil wells to understanding local markets.

For jobseekers, the key takeaway of this discussion is this: those who don't understand the changing nature of work will likely stumble into career cul-de-sacs and blind alleys, seeking work that has already been commoditized or will shortly be commoditized, at a loss as to why they can't find a job.

Once again: *your advantage is knowledge.*

What we need to understand is how both capital and labor have changed from the industrial era.

In a knowledge-based economy, capital isn't just cash or land or large-scale industrial plants. There are five types of non-financial capital that are as essential as financial capital in a knowledge-based economy. Two of these types of capital, human and social capital, are acquired by individuals through their own effort.

In the old industrial model, labor was a time-based commodity: laborers were paid for the time they spent toiling. While many low-skill jobs still pay by the hour, the hourly model no longer explains how work is valued. Higher-wage labor is not paid to perform processes that can specified and automated or offshored; Higher-wage labor is paid to *create value* and *solve problems*, and so we need to understand these two processes if we want to establish a career with higher earnings.

While knowledge and skills are obviously critical in a knowledge-based economy, knowledge is not the only factor in creating value and solving problems. We need to understand the five types of non-financial capital: human, social, cultural, symbolic and infrastructural, and work that cannot be commoditized.

These five types of capital form the *infrastructure of opportunity* described above.

These sections may require dedicated study, but it will be worth the effort: *your advantage is knowledge.*

Human and Social Capital

Human capital is an inexact term for labor's ability to take financial (money) and physical capital (tools) and create economic value. *Social capital* is the value derived from connections to others: the sum of friends, alliances, memberships and networks that create *reciprocal sources of value.* The key word here is *reciprocal,* as social capital is a two-way dynamic: it's created by providing value to others, as well as deriving value from your association with them. Reciprocity is the heart of social capital.

Within the general spectrum of human and social capital there are more subtle forms of non-material/non-financial capital, what French sociologist Pierre Bourdieu termed *cultural and symbolic capital.*

One way to give the terms more precision is to consider the example of building a house: imagine that all the necessary tools and materials are laid out on the building site, and there is a bank account with sufficient money to fund the complete construction.

Now we bring in a person with zero building experience and ask them to use the money, tools and materials to build the house solely on their own. Clearly, they will be unable to build the house because they lack the necessary *hard skills* of the building trades. They do not have the *human capital* needed to construct the house and create economic value out of the financial and material capital.

Without human capital, the financial and material capital is *dead money.* It is incapable of generating value, profit or wealth.

Suppose we enable the person to use their *soft skills* to organize others to build the house. The eight essential skills listed in the next section are the core soft skills of professionalism: being able to communicate effectively, take responsibility, be accountable, etc.

If the person lacking hard skills in building has abundant soft skills, they will be able to recruit and manage others to build the house.

This illustrates why these eight skillsets are essential: they enable anyone who owns these skills as part of their human capital to create economic value, even if they lack the applicable hard skills at the start of a project.

It is vital that we understand that these soft skills are the foundation for hard skills: if one has the eight essential soft skills, one can learn hard skills. However, note that this does not work in reverse: having hard skills does not necessarily give a person the means to acquire soft skills.

To understand *social capital,* let's imagine two scenarios.

1.	In the first case, the person tasked with building the house is given the site, cash and building materials in an unfamiliar locale where he is a complete stranger. He has no friends, contacts, group memberships or networks—he owns no social capital at all.

It's equivalent to arriving in a city and not knowing a single person.

2.	In the second scenario, the inexperienced builder is given the task in his home community, where he has friends, contacts and networks. Even if he doesn't know a single tradesperson or subcontractor, he can quickly utilize his social capital to identify trustworthy craftspeople to help him build the house.

This is like arriving in a strange city but knowing a few well-connected people: suddenly the challenges of finding a place to live, a job, some friends, etc. all become immeasurably easier.

One key aspect of human capital is overlooked in conventional descriptions of the term, which focus on knowledge and skills. But human capital isn't just skills: it's having integrity and professional standards, being trustworthy, accountable and honest. It's practicing a set of values that create economic value.

I will illustrate the importance of these elements of human capital with an example.

Let's take two people with equal levels of skill, knowledge and experience. One is a manager in a corporate or government office and the other is part of an informal alliance of free-lance professionals who work together on projects. The office is of course hierarchical and the free-lance projects are opt-in—there is no boss to give orders, every participant is equal, though each project has one key sponsor who manages the contributions of the other free-lancers.

Examples of independent free-lancers include subcontractors in the construction industry, video and audio professionals within the film industry, and writers and graphic designers in new media.

Now let's say the corporate/government manager lacks integrity and professionalism; he goes back on his word, misrepresents the views of others to benefit himself, lashes out at subordinates when he is in a foul mood, plays favorites within the office, takes credit for the work of others, misrepresents his accomplishments and cons higher management into believing he is an effective manager.

If this person were in an opt-in free-lance work environment, how many other professionals would choose to work with him? Who would willingly subject himself/herself to such a toxic sociopath who would damage the livelihoods of anyone who worked with them? One experience would be enough and the word would quickly spread: avoid this person at all costs, not because they have no skills but because they have no integrity and no professional values.

This example also highlights the downside of bureaucracies and hierarchies: bureaucratic organizations by their very nature protect the venal and the incompetent because the purpose of a bureaucracy is to diffuse accountability so that no one person is ever responsible for the organization's failure.

Human capital can only be fully valued in environments which value all aspects of human capital, not just a specific set of skills.

Human Capital as the Means of Production

If we think of human capital as something that is owned just like money or tools, we understand why author Peter Drucker wrote that workers with human capital *own the means of production in a knowledge economy*. In other words, human capital is as essential as financial or material capital.

The *means of production* are the equipment, money and expertise needed to generate goods, services and profits. In our earlier industrial economy, these were typically factories, mines, railroads, etc., assets that require a vast amount of financial capital and human labor to operate.

In the post-industrial economy, the means of production has shifted emphasis from financial capital (money) to knowledge. As the cost of the tools of production—robots and digital processing—decline, the means of production are increasingly knowledge-based.

Though post-industrial economies still need capital investment, the share of labor devoted to capital-intensive infrastructure (the electrical grid, railways, shipbuilding, etc.) declines as a percentage of total employment and economic output (gross domestic product, GDP).

Just as the percentage of the nation's capital and labor devoted to agriculture has declined precipitously (a mere 2% of the labor force now works in agriculture, down from 50% in the 19th century), so too has the percentage of the nation's workforce and capital needed to produce steel, autos, etc.

Those parts of the economy that leverage knowledge and relatively modest capital—digital media, software, 3D fabrication technology and programmable robots—have expanded their share of the economy. The more productive the sector, the more profits it generates, and this attracts more capital and talent.

The cost of the tools needed to produce high-profit goods and services is declining sharply. As a result, processes that once required costly machines and large factory spaces can increasingly be done by inexpensive desktop digital fabrication tools (e.g. 3-D printers) that cost a few thousand dollars rather than millions of dollars.

Information technologies (IT) that once required a large staff have been automated to the point where a sole proprietor can produce output on a single inexpensive computer.

In other words, the means of production in the industrial age were extremely costly factories operated by thousands of low-skilled workers. The skills, talents, experience, goals and motivation of those individual workers—their human capital—had minimal impact on the overall output of the factory (with the exception of the tool-and-die workers who made the tools).

The human capital of assembly line workers was not worth much because the work was not sensitive to skill level of the worker: a completely inexperienced worker could acquire the necessary skills in a short time. In economic terms, the worker could not charge much of a premium for his labor because his human capital had little leverage in the production of goods, services and profits. On an assembly line, a higher-skilled worker doesn't produce much more than a lower-skilled worker. The low-skill industrial worker didn't own the means of production—his economic value was limited to his time and ability to perform repetitious tasks.

Conversely, in a knowledge-based economy, the cost of human capital dwarfs the cost of machinery and tools. A desktop digital fabrication machine might cost a few thousand dollars, and the computer that runs the design software a few hundred dollars. Training the operator costs more than the tools. This is readily apparent in local government budgets, approximately 80% of which are devoted to labor costs. Though a city owns a large capital infrastructure of roads, buildings, vehicles, etc., the cost of this physical capital is considerably less than the human capital needed to operate it.

A networked economy offers new models of organizing work. An example is the open collaboration model of assembling human and social capital to complete a complex project with relatively little hierarchy and management. In this model, workers collaborate to complete a project and then move on to other work. *Crowd-sourcing*, where projects are completed by self-organizing groups of people who voluntarily join the effort is one example of this collaboration.

The financial equivalent is *crowd-funding.* In a traditional economy, anyone wanting to raise money for a new enterprise had to apply for a loan from a bank or an investment from a venture-capital fund. In the crowd-funding model, funds are raised from individuals.

The premium charged for the costly overhead of a bank or venture-capital fund vanishes; the costs of raising money have been reduced to low-cost server space and software.

Put another way, the premiums companies can charge for financial capital and hierarchical structures of production are declining. The premiums earned by the classic advantages of corporations—access to financial capital and hierarchical management—are being eroded by new networked, collaborative structures of finance and production.

The key point in this discussion of the means of production is this: the emerging economy is accelerating the value of human capital in both financial and goods-and-services producing sectors.

When we discuss *ownership of the means of production,* many observers point to the concentration of financial capital in corporations as the controlling factor: people might own their own human capital, but they have no place to invest that capital except within the confines of the state or large corporations. However, this assumption is becoming less applicable as the tools and capital needed to produce economically valuable work decline in cost, and alternatives to centralized organizations expand.

Human Capital Is Different from Financial/Material Capital

There are critical differences between human capital and financial/material capital.

1. Human capital is inherently flexible and adaptable. Indeed, one of the key attributes of human capital is that we can learn new skills and apply these to new fields. Human capital isn't just the sum total of a person's skills and knowledge—it is the ability to learn, adapt and experiment.

People who are willing to learn can keep ahead of the commoditization of labor by learning what cannot be commoditized or by moving their skills to a new field, in effect keeping ahead of commoditization.

If complexity is rewarded, we build human capital by adapting to complex workplaces. If simplicity is rewarded, we build human capital by learning how to break complexity down into simpler processes and fewer interactions.

2.   All it takes to increase human capital is time, effort and experience. Given the abundance of lessons and resources on the Internet, it requires little to no money to learn new skills other than the cost of the Internet connection.

Compare this to the arduous process of saving enough money (financial capital) to buy land or capital equipment.

While we may not be able to accumulate enough financial capital to buy costly fixed-asset means of production, flexibility and adaptability are key components of our human capital—and these are free to develop.

3.   Human capital becomes economically valuable when it *creates value* and *solves problems*. This requires *mastery* of a field, a topic we will explore later in this section. Mastery is cumulative; the more we know, the easier it is to learn more. Insights arise when expertise is applied to a new field—a process of cross-fertilization that many call *multi-disciplinary*.

Mastery and multi-disciplinary skills are generally resistant to being specified into processes that can be automated or commoditized, because mastery is an accumulation of experience that develops into a highly effective but difficult to replicate intuition. Those who have developed mastery are able to see subtleties lost on the less experienced, and can refer to a vast database of similar situations for insight into solving a particular problem.

Those with multi-disciplinary skills can apply insights from one field to another field in a process that is resistant to automation. Indeed, the point of completion—a better, cheaper, faster, more efficient way to get the same results—cannot even be specified, for the solution is not yet known.

Cultural and Symbolic Capital

Our discussion of human and social capital would be incomplete if we did not address the implicit yet often-overlooked types of capital that have termed *cultural* and *symbolic* capital. I would add a third type of capital, *infrastructural capital*.

Returning to our earlier house-building example to help illuminate these forms of capital, let's assume the building site is far from roads, rail and river transport. The task of moving the materials and to the site has suddenly become formidable. The same can be said for generating electricity to power tools, and for delivering fuel for the generator.

Mobility, electricity and transport all depend on what we might call *infrastructural capital*, the networks available to move capital and goods.

Now let's imagine that the materials have been hauled at enormous expense to the site, but the infrastructure of credit does not exist: there is no way to borrow money to pay workers to build the house. We can even imagine a scenario in which the culture lacks the conceptual (symbolic) tools necessary to create a system of credit. This is the equivalent of Western Europe before the first stirrings of modern capitalism in the 13th century.

The conceptual tools of credit are an example of symbolic capital; the cultural framework that enables those conceptual tools to become commonplace is an example of cultural capital.

If we somehow manage to accumulate financial capital in an economy that does not recognize borrowing, collateral, amortization and interest (return on capital), suppose we find the building trades are controlled by a guild. Unfortunately the guild master does not trust outsiders, so there is no way to hire local labor to build the house.

As for legal recourse—in a state with weak rule of law, there is none.

This example helps illustrate the necessary role of *infrastructural*, *cultural* and *symbolic* capital in an economy that enables the free exchange of financial, material and human/social capital.

The evolution of infrastructural, cultural and conceptual/symbolic capital has not come to an end. The emerging economy is mysterious to many because it involves developing new concepts and ways of doing things. Let's consider two examples.

> 1. In previous eras, the mechanics of someone buying 1/100th of a mortgage on a building were cumbersome. Individuals rarely had access to the information and tools needed to assess the value of the property and the risks of the loan, and so banks

performed this work for a hefty fee—the difference between the fees paid to depositors and the price the bank charged the borrower.

This is an example of *information asymmetry*, the concept that possession of knowledge that others do not have provides a significant competitive advantage. Even if individuals were able to gather the same information as banks, the mechanics of calculating and paying the monthly interest to 100 accounts was costly in time and human labor. It made practical sense to centralize the tasks in an institution (the bank) that tallied the interest and credited depositors quarterly.

In today's digital economy, there are very low cost barriers to collecting information on the building's value and the creditworthiness of the borrower, and the transactional cost of calculating and crediting the monthly interest to 100 accounts is trivial.

This example illustrates that our symbolic (i.e. conceptual) and cultural capital is evolving to enable a much more decentralized, transparent and efficient method of distributing credit, capital and risk. The value created by banks in the emerging economy is dwindling to near-zero. Indeed, in a systemic sense, the banking sector is now a parasitic, risky force in the economy, able to trigger global financial crises as a result of its excessive power while creating little of value.

2.	For our second example, let's turn to auto ownership. In the old model of private transport, in order to secure private transport, every household—and ultimately, every adult in every household—needed to buy a vehicle. This conceptual/cultural model—and the accompanying symbolism of freedom and power—created a vast industry of vehicle manufacture, fueling and maintenance.

The generation currently coming of age is significantly less attached to this model of *ownership* of private transport, as the new model of *access* to private transport is much cheaper and more flexible. However, centralized banks, manufacturers and governments still favor ownership as a model because this generates an insatiable need for credit/loans to buy the goods, a constant need to replace outdated or unfashionable models and hefty transaction/ownership taxes.

In the *access* model, full private ownership is recognized as needless and an inefficient use of capital. Why buy a car that sits unused 95% of the time?

If one hundred people can share ten vehicles that are reserved digitally and priced according to demand, this enables a much lower cost for individuals and the economy at large while also creating a new digital-technology based model for generating value and profits. This model reduces the capital expended on vehicle ownership by 90%. That also means the amount of steel and energy devoted to manufacturing and maintaining vehicles declines by 90% *with no reduction in access to private transport.*

There are additional potential gains to this open-source, crowdsourced access model. It may well be that someone borrowing a car for three hours might be able to pick up and drop off another person who then shares the cost, or pick up and drop off a parcel that is making its way to its ultimate destination via a crowdsourced route using whatever means of transport are available on the most efficient route.

These two examples illustrate how efficiencies arise from the open-sourced/crowd-sourced decentralized model.

These *social innovations* that leverage digital technologies are new forms of symbolic, conceptual and cultural capital. We can understand their eventual impact by comparing our current conceptual capital to that of a 12th century feudal society lacking in every form of cultural and symbolic capital that is essential to a modern economy. In many ways, the state-cartel centralized economy has more in common with a 12th century feudal society than it does with the emerging economy.

Mastery as the Means of Production

Familiarity with a field is rarely enough to create value and solve problems. Familiarity may be enough for low-skill commodity labor, but knowing how to create value and solve problems requires *mastery*, for only mastery generates a premium. In the context of the previous section, we can define mastery as *owning the means of production in a knowledge economy*, for mastery is a key component of human capital. All the other components of human capital—flexibility, adaptability, self-discipline, learning how to learn, etc.—serve the goal of attaining economically valuable mastery.

Consider the case of an experienced handyperson who can troubleshoot and repair dozens of different problems in dwellings. The hand tools needed to perform the majority of these repairs are mass-produced and relatively inexpensive. The financial and material capital needed to create value as a handyperson is modest; the largest capital expense is transport to various jobs.

By themselves, these tools cannot possibly create any economic value; they are useless. In the hands of an inexperienced, low-skill worker, they will more likely be a force of value destruction rather than value creation. *Only in the hands of an experienced, skilled knowledge worker can the tools create value.*

The apprentice handyperson will lack the experience and skills to quickly and correctly assess the problem and determine the lowest-cost, most efficient means to repair the problem. The less skilled worker may well take five times as long to make the repair as the worker who has mastered all the required trades, and may well select repair options that cost more and are less effective.

In other words, mastery—deep expertise based on experience and *ownership of the work*—is the key element to value creation. Mastery is what creates a premium for human capital.

Mastery is not just a mix of knowledge, expertise and experience: it also requires *ownership of the work*, meaning that the master performs all work as if he owns every aspect of it: the process, the final product and the reputation that arises from the work.

The worker who does not own their work is careless and slipshod, an attitude expressed in phrases such as "close enough for government work," or "there's no point it doing it right, nobody else does." The worker who owns knowledge and expertise but is incapable of owning their work can never achieve mastery.

It is vital that we understand that mastery is not just a collection of hard skills; it is also a value system of ownership of all work, no matter how menial it may appear to the outsider. In a very real sense, the worker who doesn't own his work does not really own the means of production.

To illustrate the mindset of mastery, let's consider garden maintenance as an example. The master gardener treats each of the yards in his care as if he owned it, and as if every aspect of his care is a reflection of his reputation and skill. It doesn't matter if the garden's owner is rich or poor or pleasant or unpleasant; the work is done equally well for all because the master gardener owns all his work equally.

To establish and maintain a livelihood in the emerging economy, students must be able to build economically valuable mastery in their chosen field. Simply acquiring generalized knowledge will not be enough to create value.

In traditional economies, mastery is gained by serving a long unpaid apprenticeship with a master craftsperson. The master often owns his/her own workshop, and provides the apprentices with room and board. In exchange for years of hard labor, the master teaches the apprentices the processes and skills of the craft. Such apprentice-master craftsperson arrangements still exist in the traditional handcrafts of Japan.

Creating Value and the Matrix of Work

I have repeatedly described higher-value work as work that *creates value* and *solves problems*. To help differentiate between lower-value work that completes tasks and higher value work, we turn to three measures that together form what I call the *matrix of work*.

We can think of each measure as a spectrum or sliding scale: the lower the work is on the scale, the less value it creates. The higher the work is on the spectrum, the more value it creates. When we overlay these three measures, we have an insightful way to measure the value of work.

We've already covered the first measure: how much of the work is *process-based*? As we've seen, the point of completion and each step of the way can be specified in process-based work, and this makes it programmable and tradable: process-based work can be automated or offshored, i.e. commoditized.

Non-process-based work cannot be specified because the solution is not yet known.

The second measure is the value is derived from empathy, compassion, touch and emotional support. This work is intrinsically non-programmable because the value is not created by a process but by a human connection. Though offshore workers can interact with each other via videoconferencing, and a robot can be programmed to mimic a human smile, digital and machine facsimiles of empathy are not interchangeable with authentic human empathy and caring.

Since the core attribute of commoditization is interchangeability, work that derives its value from human connections cannot be commoditized.

I call this measure *high-touch/low-touch*. Interactions in which human connections constitute much of the economic value are at the high end of the *high touch/low touch* spectrum. An example of low touch is shopping online, where the processes and interactions are automated. Examples of high-touch include medical care, mentoring, sales and psychotherapy.

Some types of high touch work are relatively low-skill (for example, assisted living aide), while others require high levels of knowledge and experience (for example, psychiatrist). The value isn't created by skill level but by the ability to give someone your full attention and form an emotional bond of empathy, compassion and respect.

The third measure is the sensitivity of the work output to experience and mastery. I am indebted to writer Michael O. Church for his explanation of the difference between work that is insensitive to mastery and work that is highly sensitive to mastery. He describes these two classes of work as *convex* and *concave*, a terminology derived from charting skill-based experience to output. One type of work is relatively insensitive to higher skills and deeper experience, while the other is sensitive to high levels of skill and experience, i.e. mastery.

We can understand the distinction by asking this question: which step leads to the biggest leap in productivity, the step from beginner to enough experience to work independently, or the step from being able to work independently to a high level of skill and experience, i.e. mastery?

If the qualitative and quantitative difference between beginners and moderately experienced workers is significant, and the difference in output between workers with some experience and those with many years of experience is minimal, this is the first type.

If the qualitative and quantitative difference between beginners and moderately experienced workers is modest, and the difference in output between the moderately experienced workers and those with many years of experience is significant, this is the second type.

Where is the big leap in productivity—between beginners and those with 6 months of experience, or between those with six months of experience and those with six years of experience? Where does additional experience and skill no longer yield any increase in productivity? Does additional experience increase productivity over an entire career? Answering these questions helps identify the limitations of work that is learned relatively quickly but which is insensitive to further gains in skills.

In our yard maintenance example, a worker with some experience is significantly more productive at mowing the lawn than the beginner. But a master gardener with years of experience isn't much faster at mowing the lawn than the low-skill worker.

In *convex work*, the difference in productivity between the beginner and the worker with some experience is insignificant but the difference between middling experience and mastery is large. Writing software is often used as an example of convex work, as the learning curve is steep enough that workers with some experience are not much more productive than beginners, while the highly skilled workers are significantly more productive than workers with some experience and skills.

In fields that depend heavily on creativity or innovation, the economic value of the work done by the most experienced workers is many times higher than that of moderately experienced workers.

On other words, is the work *experiential-sensitive*?

Some skills can be gained relatively quickly while others require a long apprenticeship. While we tend to associate long learning curves with fields such as medicine and law that are widely assumed to be impervious to automation, some aspects of these specialized fields are being automated, for example, primary screening in electrocardiography. Though we assume skills that are difficult to master cannot be performed by machines, this overlooks the critical distinction between specialized knowledge that is *process-based* (i.e. the specialized knowledge is only needed once to set up the process) versus work that requires the flexible application of experience that cannot be reduced to a repeatable routine.

Locating tumors on x-rays, for example, is a high-skill task that is largely specifiable and can be performed by a machine. Unlike a human, the machine doesn't get tired and is thus less likely to make errors in the screening process.

The preparation of many legal documents is also process-based: once the template is set so that it complies with applicable regulations, a low-skill worker or the customer can provide the input.

Many professions have digitized their process-based expertise into computer programs that are not available to the general public; the cost of operating the program is low, but the professionals charge a high fee because the product must be validated by the preparer. Examples include income tax returns, real estate appraisals and legal documents such as incorporation papers.

In other words, the work has already been automated but the high cost to the customer does not reflect this, as the validation by the preparer establishes an artificial scarcity value. For example, real estate appraisal software generates appraisals for a very low cost, but the validation by the licensed appraiser creates a scarcity value because the number of licensed appraisers is limited.

On the other end of the *process-based* scale, learning to treat patients with a friendly, caring manner while performing low-skilled labor is relatively easy to learn, but this high-touch value cannot be entirely replaced by a machine.

Some studies have found that people respond positively to robots that mimic human signifiers of caring, so it may be that robots with higher-touch capabilities will begin to replace high-touch human workers. Whether we approve of this or not is beside the point; if the quality of care increases and costs decrease, this trend will accelerate.

The *process-based /experiential-sensitive* categories are not necessarily either/or. For example, welding is a difficult skill to master. In process-based work such as standardized parts moving down an assembly line, a robot welder is much faster and more accurate than a human welder. In customized, one-off work, however, the human welder and the welding robot become a complementary team; the robot handles the welding that it is optimized to do, and the human does the welding that it is impractical for the robot perform.

The unifying characteristics of work that is difficult to automate are *mastery of skills that cannot be specified into repeatable processes, flexibility and high touch.* These skills—along with the eight essential skills—are key characteristics of human and social capital.

Why does this matter to jobseekers? Let's take the example of someone learning to install drywall. The beginner is not very productive, while the worker with six months experience is very productive. The worker with six years' experience is not much faster than the one with six months' experience, though he will likely know more about custom situations than the worker with six months experience.

The problem for the worker is that the value he can create (and therefore his wage) hits the top of the S-Curve in six months; he is already at or near his maximum earning power. Accumulating more experience won't increase his earnings unless he learns an additional trade or learns to manage a crew, that is, acquires new fields of knowledge that will increase the value of his skills/human capital.

To understand the S-Curve of value creation and earnings potential, we need to explore the concept of *premium*, i.e. how work creates value.

The Premium of Labor

Let's start with the three fundamental components of the economy:

1. the free market

2. the state (government)

3. the community, i.e. all the activity and assets that are not priced by the market or controlled by the state. Examples include churches, neighborhood groups and non-profit organizations. These interact with both the market and state, but the purpose of the organization is not to reap a profit or enforce regulations and laws.

In the free market economy, revenues must exceed expenses, i.e. the enterprise must generate a profit. Costs include

- materials,

- labor and overhead (labor overhead includes employer's tax payments, unemployment insurance, etc., while general overhead includes office rent, accounting, etc.),

- capital investment (replacing or upgrading equipment and software)

If the enterprise loses money, it will eventually close, or bankrupt whatever entity is subsidizing the losses. As author Peter Drucker noted, enterprises do not have profits, they only have expenses. If the costs of producing the good or service exceed the market value of the product, production costs must be reduced or the enterprise will lose money and shut down.

The current global economy is characterized by over-capacity: the supply of goods and services is larger than the demand. There are too many steel mills, hotel rooms, factories making TVs, etc., and relatively few manufactured goods that are scarce. This forces enterprises to reduce their input costs—the costs of production—to reap a profit.

In many cases, labor is the most expensive component of production costs. Labor must generate a premium, a gain in value beyond the cost of the labor. For example, if a company pays an employee an annual salary of $40,000, the firm must also pay labor overhead and benefits, costs which may add 50% to the base wage. The company must also generate a gross profit large enough to fund capital investment, general overhead and a return on the capital invested in the enterprise.

Thus a worker paid $40,000 must generate $100,000 of economic value to justify his employment.

Since a robot and its digital software do not need healthcare, unemployment and disability insurance or a pension plan, the robot costs 50% less than the human worker even if the robot's operational costs equals the base wage paid to the human worker.

As the costs of digital technology fall and the ability of this technology to replace human labor increases, the premium generated by labor declines: if a robot that costs $20,000 a year to operate can replace a human worker being paid $40,000, the value of the human labor falls to the robot's operational cost, i.e. $20,000 per year. *Labor that cannot be replaced by software/machines generates a premium, especially if the labor is in a sector where prices are high due to scarcity of the good or service being produced.*

Outside of cartels that fix the price of their products, the market dictates the scarcity/abundance and supply/demand for goods, services and labor. When there is an oversupply of goods, services and labor, the price of all three falls.

As the number of jobs that cannot be replaced by technology declines, the supply of labor increases. This supply and demand imbalance tends to drive wages down, as more workers compete for increasingly scarce jobs.

We need to distinguish between a premium and a subsidy. If the government pays above-market wages, it doesn't mean the state's labor force is creating a premium; it simply means the taxpayers are subsidizing the state workers' higher pay.

Let's take state-mandated labor at gasoline stations as an example. Some states require that gasoline must be pumped by paid staff rather than by the customers. This is a policy decision that creates jobs that would not exist if customers pumped their own gasoline. The jobs are subsidized by buyers of gasoline (and perhaps taxpayers; the details vary from state to state).

There is a premium generated by someone pumping gasoline for customers, but the premium is only as large as what customers willingly pay extra for the service. If having gasoline pumped for you costs 10% more in the open market, then that is the premium labor creates for that service. Any sum beyond that is a subsidy.

Ultimately, all state subsidies are paid by the surplus generated by non-state workers and enterprises. That means there is a limit on how much the state can subsidize labor. The Federal government could print unlimited sums of money, but eventually this will cripple the economy. (For more on this, please see my book *Why Things Are Falling Apart and What We Can Do About It*.)

In the free market, labor can charge a premium if it is scarce (i.e. few people have the necessary skills) or it creates high value in the marketplace. As noted earlier, *mastery of skills that cannot be fully specified as repeatable processes, flexibility and high touch* create economic value.

Conversely, if the skills are not scarce and/or the value created is low, the wages will also be low. This is why fast-food preparation is paid modest wages. The work is hard and fast-paced but doesn't require high skills, so the value created is relatively low. How much premium are people willing to pay to be served fast food by a human worker? We can ask the same question of retail purchases. Many people like being served by a human and will pay a premium for this service. Others would prefer to order online or be served by a machine if the cost is lower.

Being served fast food is low touch; there is little value in the human interaction. The workers are interchangeable, the definition of commoditized labor. In general, people won't pay premiums for low touch interactions, and so these processes are prone to being automated.

Since one fast-food meal is relatively similar to other fast-food meals, there is little premium placed on the skill of the preparer. Low touch, low skill work has little premium, so the benefits of automation are compelling to employers facing ever-higher labor overhead costs in an economy burdened with over-capacity.

In contrast, a restaurant can offer a high-touch, high-skill experience and thus it can charge a premium for its ambience, serve staff and freshly prepared meals. The labor generates the premium: a restaurant with an abundance of ambience will soon be deserted if the staff is incompetent and the food poorly prepared.

Some labor generates its value less from specialized skills and more from high touch. These workers do not need lengthy skills-based training to create value; the value is created by high touch characteristics such as empathy and the professionalism embodied by the eight essential skills.

As we have seen, there are three sources of value creation. The higher the worker's level, the larger the premium his/her labor can generate:

1.	process-based/not process-based

2.	low-touch / high-touch

3.	experiential sensitivity, i.e. the sensitivity of output to mastery

It's important to note that these sources of value do not necessarily align with the driver of higher earnings in the pre-software/robotics era: specialization. The key to higher earnings in the past was to specialize in one narrow field, as relatively few people would possess expertise in that specialty. The narrower the division of labor, the thinking went, the more productive the specialist and the higher the value of his labor.

But since specialized skills may well be more reducible to a process than generalized knowledge, specialization is not necessarily a panacea. There are other problems with specialization. One is that the narrower the field, the more vulnerable it is to changes in the market that render it obsolete.

Another is that the vast higher education industry has sought to market specialized advanced degrees as the solution to diploma inflation and the decreasing value of a college degree. One can now get a master's degree, for example, in casino management. Though this specialization promises some narrow expertise that might create a premium if there is a shortage of people with casino management experience, it becomes an albatross if no such demand exists: a specialized degree simply gives prospective employers a handy reason to reject the candidate as unqualified.

The takeaway here is that specialization no longer guarantees a premium for labor. Skills that are sensitive to mastery are difficult to specify and turn into a process, regardless of whether they are specialized or generalized. Specialization by itself does not confer resistance to commoditization.

What creates a premium in the emerging economy is professionalism, adaptability, skills that can be applied to new fields (i.e. cross-pollination)

and the ability to learn new skills.

Creating Value with Human and Social Capital

I have stressed that the purpose of work is to create value and solve problems. In this section, we look at two small-scale examples of how value is created in the emerging economy with *social innovation.*

Studies have found that human creativity is largely the result of sharing ideas and transferring innovations in one field to other fields. Innovation may arise from a single person, but its application requires human and social capital.

The two small-scale examples described below illustrate how human and social capital works in conjunction with infrastructure, community and financial capital.

Example 1: Farming as currently practiced is overwhelmingly industrial, and few would see any application of knowledge to the sector as being useful except to further the mechanization/automation of agribusiness. Yet highly educated people are profitably truck farming by applying their knowledge of marketing, food preparation and the restaurant business. For example, the trend-setting restaurant Chez Panisse in Berkeley, Calif., has a supply network of small farms, which in some cases are run by former employees of the restaurant. These small farmers are paid a good price for supplying very fresh organic produce. What is delivered daily sets the restaurant's menu for that day's lunch and dinner.

The key value creation in this arrangement is trust (social capital), attention to quality, and the ability to fashion menus around a variety of seasonal produce and meats (human capital). The labor of raising the produce is essential but it alone doesn't create the value.

Example 2: Street-Level Cycles in Berkeley, Calif., is an organization that partners long-abandoned city property with private enterprise to offer classes in bicycle repair and free use of the shop's tools to do-it-yourselfers who want to repair their own bikes. It also provides bike repair services and sells used bicycles. The income generated by the repair service and sales of used bikes supports a small staff and enables the free community use of the shop's tools.

The amount of financial capital needed to start this enterprise was modest. The city-owned building was unoccupied for years. In exchange for use of the property, the city gets a self-funding, free community educational resource and service. The enterprise serves a wide spectrum of the community: students, do-it-yourselfers, those needing bike repairs or an inexpensive used bicycle. In offering the free classes to students, the enterprise has no competitors. In selling repair services and used bikes, it competes with other local bike shops. If someone wants to learn how to repair bicycles, this organization offers a nexus of tools and opportunities to learn and practice.

This low-cost synergy of local government, private enterprise, education, community service and social and human capital did not require any technological innovation—it required social innovation. It illustrates that the profit motive—often held up as the only motivator within capitalism—is not the only motivation for either innovation or enterprise.

These small-scale examples illustrate that innovation often takes what already exists in terms of financial and infrastructure capital and combines these ideas and resources into new methods of value creation. They also show that the key role of human and social capital in creating value via social innovation does not necessarily require more financial or infrastructure capital—and indeed may require less. This can be summarized as *doing more with less*.

Value creation and problem-solving arise from many sources, not just the technological innovations that receive media coverage. If we combine the many sources of value creation unleashed by digital technologies, we realize that ours is one of the great transformative eras in human history.

Alienation and Work

In Marx's view, workers were alienated from the product of their work because they did not own the product or control the means of production. Marx argued that the absence of ownership and control was also an absence of agency (control of one's destiny) and meaning. Workers were estranged from the product of their work, from other workers and from themselves, as the natural order of the product of work belonging to the one who produced it was upended by capitalism.

Marx characterized this separation of work from ownership of the work and its output as social alienation from human nature. Capitalism, in his view, did not just reorder production into enterprises whose sole goal was profit and accumulating more capital; it destroyed the natural connection between the worker, the processes of work and the output or product of his work.

Marx was thus one of the first to analyze work not just in terms of economic output but in social and psychological terms.

This tradition was carried on by writers such as Eric Hoffer, who saw work as the source of life's meaning, and Christopher Lasch, who saw the rise of consumerism as the basis of meaning and the rootless cosmopolitanism of the modern economy as the source of a culture of narcissism. For Lasch, the relentless commoditization of life disrupted the natural social relations of family, social reciprocity and the workplace, depriving individuals of these sources of meaning and replacing them with an empty consumerism that worshipped fame and celebrity.

The marketplaces' commoditization of everyday life—both parents working all day for corporations so they could afford corporate childcare, for example—created two alienating dynamics: a narcissistic personality crippled by a fragile sense of self that sought solace in consumerist identifiers (wearing the right brands, etc.) and a therapeutic mindset that saw alienation not as the consequence of large-scale, centralized commoditization and financialization but as individual issues to be addressed with self-help and pop psychology.

In Lasch's view, both of these dynamics ignored the loss of authenticity that resulted from the commoditization not just of production but of every aspect of everyday life. In this sense, Lasch's social analysis is an extension of Marx's original insight into the alienating dynamics of commoditized wage-work, in which workers and their work were both interchangeable.

Lasch's analysis brings us to the source of modern alienation: it's not just employees who are interchangeable—employers are equally interchangeable. The interchangeability of work, employees, employers, products and services is the key characteristic of commoditization.

What is the takeaway for those seeking a job or career? There are several takeaways.

One is that the sources of value creation are linked to the level of agency (control of one's work) and ownership of the work: work that is not process-based (i.e. that cannot be commoditized) and that is experientially sensitive to mastery enables a higher level of agency and ownership because the worker owns the means of production—his human and social capital.

The second is that the dramatic lowering of barriers to education and the ownership of tools powered by the Internet has greatly expanded the opportunities to escape an alienating dependence on the state and cartels for employment and on superficial consumerism for meaning.

If we trust networks rather than states or corporations for our security, we automatically gain agency (control of our work and lives) and an authentic sense of self gained from owning our work and the results of our work.

It is important to understand that corporations exist to make a profit and accumulate capital, for if they do not make a profit and accumulate capital they will bleed capital and disappear. To believe that organizations dedicated to making a profit could magically organize society in ways that benefit every participant is nonsense. Corporations organize labor and capital to accumulate capital. It is absurd to expect that such organized self-interest magically optimizes the social order. This is not to blame all the ills of society on corporations; it is simply to note that corporations are limited by their limited purpose. Their purpose is not to organize a healthy, sustainable economy; it is to organize labor and capital in such a way that the corporation can accumulate capital in a marketplace controlled by supply and demand of the present.

Corporations have profited greatly from the alienation of work and the social order, as narcissistic debt-based consumerism is a highly profitable economic order, even if it is socially dysfunctional, unsustainable and destructive to individual agency and meaning.

We conclude this section on the changing nature of work by noting that the expansion of decentralized, distributed networks, the near-zero cost of knowledge and the declining cost of the means of production (digital memory and processors, software, 3-D fabrication machines, robots and tools) offer newfound opportunities for workers to reclaim their agency and ownership of their work and output.

Rather than rely on centralized states and corporations to organize labor and capital, collaborative networks can do so without alienating workers from their work and disrupting the sources of meaning.

The changing economy is opening up new ways to reconnect workers to their work and the profits from their work. These include traditional models such as self-employment and worker-owned cooperatives and new models of collaborative project-based work.

How do we change a dysfunctional, unsustainable and alienating system?

By creating new ways of creating value and alternative models of cooperative work and ownership of the means of production.

Corporations and the state will have to adapt by offering workers more agency and ownership, or they will slide down the S-Curve to decay or collapse. *Those sectors not busy being born are busy dying.*

Section Three: The Core Skills and Values That Create Economic Value

The Eight Essential Skills of Professionalism

What makes a worker a professional? In the conventional use of the word, professionalism means membership in a profession that is defined by a license to practice a specific trade.

I am using *professionalism* in a much broader sense, to describe those attributes that enable a worker to be productive in their own work and work effectively with others.

I have distilled these attributes into eight core skills.

One would think that professionalism—broadly speaking, the ability to self-manage, to be accountable, to communicate clearly, learn new material and work easily with others—would be a core curriculum in higher education, given its critical importance in the world of work. One would be wrong.

Professionalism is not taught or even recognized as a subject worthy of being taught. Rather, the current educational system assumes that students learn these skills by osmosis or magic.

What do I mean by osmosis or magic? *Critical skills are not taught directly, they are assumed to be transferred via standard coursework.* For example, *self-learning to mastery* is one of the essential skills needed to thrive in the emerging economy (skills 1 and 2 below). The current system assumes that taking conventional courses teaches everyone to learn on one's own to the point of mastery. But like every other skill, the ability to self-learn to mastery must be explicitly taught and learned.

The current system assumes that classroom interactions impart the interpersonal skills needed to work effectively with others in the workplace, but it is quite possible to earn high marks in higher education and exit the system with poor interpersonal skills.

It is assumed that successfully navigating the institutions of higher education will impart professional skills: showing up on time, performing as promised, being accountable, and so on. Once again, this assumption is false: *performing well in institutions of higher learning has no correlation to performance in the workplace.*

If the higher education system does not explicitly teach these skills, students will not learn them, even if they excel in fulfilling the criteria of higher education—earning high marks on exams, etc.

The unspoken assumption of the current higher education system is "we're not a trade school; it's up to employers to teach their new employees." This is yet more evidence that higher education is completely out of touch with the real-world economy: in the real world, employers want new employees who are able to create value by *profitably solving problems* on Day One. Training people to be professional is a waste of time and money to enterprises facing a surplus of college-educated applicants.

The ultimate purpose of skills is to *solve problems.* Problem-solving has become a cliché of sorts, and so we need to ask, what set of skills is required to profitably solve problems?

The set of necessary skills divides into two categories: *hard skills* in specific fields and *soft skills* that enable *ownership of tasks and projects*, systematic application of creativity and critical thinking, and professional standards of collaboration and conduct.

These two sets of skills are essential parts of *human and social capital*, the matrix of applied knowledge, hard and soft skills, experience and the ability to work productively with others. The ultimate purpose of education is to learn how to acquire human and social capital, and the ultimate purpose of human and social capital is mastery of the skills needed to solve problems.

Problem-solving and *accountability* have been generalized to the point that we need to specify what they actually mean. In my terminology, they mean taking ownership of tasks and projects, i.e. accepting sole responsibility in the same manner as an owner.

Hard skills in the STEM subjects (science, technology, engineering and math) are no longer enough: professional collaboration skills are increasingly essential even in workplaces that require engineering and scientific proficiency. The *soft skills* of collaboration, adaptability, creativity, entrepreneurism and professional accountability are core skills in every sector of the emerging economy.

The skills of professionalism are not learned by osmosis or magic; they must be taught as systematically as hard skills.

The skills needed to establish and maintain a livelihood in the emerging economy are the abilities to:

1. Learn challenging new material over one's entire productive life

2. Creatively apply newly-mastered knowledge and skills to a variety of fields

3. Be adaptable, responsible and accountable in all work environments

4. Apply a full spectrum of entrepreneurial skills to any task, i.e. take ownership of one's work

5. Work collaboratively and effectively with others, both in person and remotely (online)

6. Communicate clearly and effectively in all work environments

7. Continually build human and social capital, i.e. knowledge and networks

8. Possess a practical working knowledge of financial records and project management

If we step back and consider the soft skills needed to succeed in the emerging economy, we marvel that anyone believes the prevailing (but unspoken) assumption that coursework in the conventional fields of language, history, science and the humanities magically instills these essential skills in students via the regurgitation of mass-produced coursework.

Hard skills and the soft skills of professionalism are only two-thirds of what's needed to establish and maintain a livelihood; a productive value system is just as essential as a set of skills.

Values as the Incubator of Economic Value

Our higher education system is based on the conviction that the primary impediment to universal prosperity is a lack of knowledge, which can be remedied with more education. This conviction cuts across ideological lines, as virtually everyone declares their belief in the economic value of education.

Since the key to prosperity is increasing productivity, the question becomes: does increasing a person's knowledge make them more productive?

In some cases, the answer is clearly yes, but in other cases the answer is just as clearly no. Though it is politically sensitive, the difference between these two is based on the individual's value system and habits of behavior and thought.

The key traits needed not just to learn effectively but to apply the knowledge productively are self-discipline, the ability to focus for long periods of time, set aside current gratification for longer-term goals, persevere through difficulty and failure, work with others, accept responsibility and remain accountable at all times, along with a desire to achieve mastery in the skills required to secure a livelihood. All of this requires some self-knowledge and self-confidence.

This *ecosystem of values* is established early in life within the family and community. It is not unique to any one culture, society or faith; it is universal and accessible to all. Becoming a productive person is not limited to any one sector of the economy, or any one level of native intelligence. Though these values and habits are first acquired (or not acquired) in the family and community, they can be acquired later in life if the student is willing to learn.

A large body of research supports this common-sense connection between the core values acquired in the home and future prosperity. For example, the quantity and variety of books in the household is a better predictor of students' test scores than household income. Though wealthier families have the financial resources to offer their children more enrichment (after-school classes, for example), the immigrant experience in America provides countless examples of families arriving with no financial assets who manage by dint of unceasing effort and thrift to lift their children into the prosperous class of highly productive citizens.

Conventional education assumes these values will be absorbed by osmosis; unfortunately there is little evidence for this osmosis theory, and plenty of evidence that the gap between those with these values and those lacking these values widens in school rather than narrows. Economists Pedro Carneiro and James Heckman concluded: "Differences in cognitive and noncognitive skills by family income and family background emerge early and persist. If anything, schooling widens these early differences."

In other words, conventional education benefits those who already possess the values and qualities that make them educable.

There are several factors in these differences. Educated parents clearly value education, as their own behavior reinforces the commitment to pursue higher education. Emotionally nurturing parents and caregivers instill the self-confidence needed to persevere through failure and criticism, and a culturally nurturing family provides the intellectual stimulation and human capital of early exposure to music, religion, the arts, positive ethnic identity and exposure to the social capital of cultural institutions.

As Jerry Muller wrote in his 2013 essay *Capitalism and Inequality*, "Each generation of social scientists discovers anew (and much to their chagrin), the resources transmitted by the family tend to be highly determinative of success in school and the workplace."

There is little mystery about what separates accomplished, successful and prosperous families from those who struggle financially. The accomplished families are invariably led by parents who lead by example. Parents who play a musical instrument for pleasure reveal the payoff for the hard work of learning to play music, and those who serve on church or community committees illustrate the satisfaction and benefits of serving others. Parents who pursue interests and improve their own mastery outside of school or the workplace pass these values on to their children.

Additionally, though one would not know it from mainstream media coverage, financial wealth is still linked causally to the values of thrift and productive use of capital. Remarkably, developing human and social capital does not necessarily require wealth or high income. Rather, a key determinant of human capital (psychological resilience, self-confidence and emotional intelligence) is the amount of nurturing time parents spend with their children and the parents' expectations of their children's behavior and values.

Mainstream financial and social success depends on networks and connections—social capital that is enabled by human capital. Those with more human capital are better able to take advantage of opportunities to build social capital than those with minimal human capital. The real advantage of attending an elite university is not the quality of the instruction per se but the opportunities to form friendships and professional connections that open doors unavailable to those outside the elite university. In other words, it is the social capital that counts, not the knowledge gained.

However, it requires an abundance of human capital to exploit these opportunities: the social skills of knowing how to dress and interact with accomplished people, knowing how to present (but not oversell) oneself, possessing the broad cultural knowledge necessary to understand the terms and contexts of conversations and situations, the self-confidence and humility needed to be a beginner, being a good listener, being able to recruit a mentor, gracefully accepting criticism, and so on.

Little of this human capital is related to one's educational level or classroom knowledge. If creativity is causally linked to the networking of creative people and new ideas, then one's network is more of a determinant of success than educational attainment per se – and research supports this contention.

The goal of human and social capital is to develop what I term *network intelligence*: the creativity and connections that arise from participating in productive networks. The upper-class family is wealthy not just in assets, but in social capital, connections that open doors or solve problems in ways that are unavailable to the less well-connected.

If the family establishes our basic human and social capital, then what role does education play, other than widening the existing gaps between those with more and less human/social capital? It is my contention that education can only increase productivity and the acquisition of human and social capital in two ways: (1) helping students learn how to learn, making the student the teacher; and (2) explicitly teaching the values, behaviors and habits that are needed to build human and social capital.

This is an old story, of course: give a man a fish and you feed him for a day; teach him how to fish and he will feed himself for a lifetime. This is not just a matter of providing knowledge; it also requires an understanding of the essential role of values and human and social capital.

Those lacking the necessary values can learn how to acquire them. With those values, behaviors and habits in hand, acquiring human and social capital becomes not just possible but inevitable.

Investing in Ourselves

How do we acquire values and habits that manifest those values in our everyday lives? The key was described by Aristotle in ancient times: *We are what we repeatedly do.* Put another way: *We are what we do every day.* This explains the importance of habits, which are habits precisely because we do them every day or week, repeating the process again and again.

I am generally skeptical of the value of behavioral economics, as the primary insight (that humans are irrational and rationalize their mistakes/failures) doesn't differentiate between economic systems that function positively for most participants (i.e. low rates of corruption and inequality, high levels of liberty and transparency) and those which fail most participants. In other words, since all participants in both systems are prone to irrationality, how do beneficial systems arise? Behavioral economics is silent on systems, and that severely limits its utility in my view.

I also find little practical value in the insight that we overvalue ourselves when we succeed and rationalize our failures (we didn't have enough resources, etc.), as these irrationalities have been selected over time because they serve a positive function in maintaining our self-confidence.

The insight of behavioral economics that has a practical application is the awareness that our will-power/self-discipline is a limited resource which we must invest wisely. In this sense it is a form of scarce capital—what I call *willpower capital*. I liken it to a pool fed by a spring: when we exert our self-discipline, we drain the supply of willpower. Given time, the pool will replenish itself. But once we've drained our available self-discipline, tasks that require self-discipline become much more taxing.

When we invest our *willpower capital* in an organized fashion to developing new processes (habits), we are *investing in ourselves*.

We can distill the dynamics of changing our habits to express positive values into five points:

     1.   It requires a daily application of self-discipline to form a new habit or replace a destructive habit with a more positive one.

     2.   If we spend our available willpower on an array of projects rather than on developing one new habit, we are unlikely to be able to persevere long enough to cement that new habit to the point where it is part of our routine.

     3.   The earlier in the day we apply our self-discipline to forming a new habit, the more success we will have simply because our reserves of willpower are most abundant early in the day.

     4.   Setting goals is easy. What's difficult is *developing a process to reach the goal*, and making that process into a habit that becomes part of our routine.

     5.   Once a process becomes habit, we don't need to invest as much *willpower capital* in maintaining it.

The power to shape what we repeatedly do is the power to become more professional, improve our productivity, learn new material every day, and become a better mentor, more compassionate, a better listener— whatever we set as goals.

It's not surprising that many of the most productive people (artists, writers, scientists, etc.) often rise early and put in a solid morning of work without distraction. Given the nature of willpower and habit, that schedule makes good sense.

It is human nature to over-estimate our role in success and blame the system for our failures, and to focus on what we can't control rather than what we can control. Our economy is dysfunctional and structurally flawed; the centralized systems that dominate our economy are all on the diminishing return/decline phase of the S-Curve. (I have described these systemic flaws in a number of my books.) As individuals, we can't fix these systemic failures. We have to live in the economy we have, not the one we hope will evolve in the future. What we do control is our own professionalism, values, integrity, authenticity, knowledge, skills and human and social capital.

Working Knowledge of Financial Records and Project Management

You may have noticed that seven of the eight core skills are *soft skills* and only the last one, a practical working knowledge of financial records and project management, is a *hard skill*. I included this hard skill because it is the foundation of assessing and organizing work that creates value or solves problems.

I did not use the word *accounting* because that word scares those who associate it with a difficult, tedious math-heavy slog. But the reality is that keeping accurate financial records and understanding what they communicate is necessary not just for large organizations but for farmers' markets, bike repair shops, community groups, sole proprietors, etc.—every organization and enterprise.

The math required to maintain accurate financial records is simple addition and subtraction. It is not difficult.

The key characteristic of useful financial records is separating expenses and income into practical categories. Basic accounting software (for example, checkbook-balancing programs) enables users to attach a code to separate different categories of expenses and income. For example, utilities such as electrical bills and mobile phone charges might be coded 101. Restaurant and fast-food meals might be 102, and so on.

Humans are not wired to keep accurate accounts in their minds, and as a result, people with no accurate financial records are generally surprised to discover exactly how much they spend on groceries or eating out.

Why do accurate financial records matter? They are an essential component in understanding a problem well enough to actually solve it, and they are the foundation of effective project management.

If you come across an organization in chaos, you will inevitably find that the financial records are equally chaotic or that those in charge cannot understand the financial records and are thus unable to understand the organization's problems or the practicality of proposed solutions.

To solve problems, we must first understand the nature of the problem, and assess what resources are available to address the problem. Financial records help us accomplish both tasks. One part of our assessment is a cost-benefit analysis: how much will the proposed solution cost, and what is the *opportunity cost* of that solution? The opportunity cost is what was left undone because the available resources were devoted to the chosen project. Making the wrong choice and devoting resources to the wrong solution could doom the organization.

To calculate the opportunity cost, we must prepare a realistic budget for each option. Only then can we make an informed decision.

For those with no financial reporting experience, one place to start is your own household's income and expenses. Online courses and tutorials are resources available to anyone with a n Internet connection. The goal is to become familiar with income and expense sheets, also called profit and loss statements (P&L) and balance sheets which track assets and liabilities. These are the standard formats for reporting the finances of any organization.

Every project also has a financial reporting backbone: the budget, which compares projected expenses and income with actual expenses and income.

Ultimately, all work can be viewed as a project with a budget and a profit or loss. Everything from a home garden to a garage workshop to a global division can be constructively viewed as a project with a goal and a structure designed to reach that goal.

Developing a working knowledge of project management is thus the core skill needed to oversee and participate in any work, and understanding financial reporting is a key component in managing any project of any size.

As noted earlier, the two dynamics that characterize decline and eventual failure are diminishing returns and the S-Curve. Unproductive investments are those that absorb more and more resources while yielding less and less output: this is the classic definition of diminishing returns. But any project that wastes resources or makes inefficient use of resources is also guaranteeing diminishing returns.

The core of project management is establishing appropriate metrics to measure effectiveness, cost and opportunity cost, and to fully understand what the metrics are communicating. Financial reporting provided one metric, and measuring input and output is another. These are the core skills of good project management.

For example, if the project is designing a website for customers, the site's utility is measured not just by how much it cost to develop but by the quality and reliability of the user experience. A site whose functionality is limited or that crashes constantly is simply not effective: the output is substandard.

If a classroom project absorbs a tremendous amount of resources but does not result in improving measurable student learning, the project's output is substandard.

Effective project management requires:

1. Accountability

2. Transparency

3. Shared information and feedback (i.e. no *information hoarding* is allowed)

4. Each piece of the project is small enough that failures can be resolved without threatening the progress of the entire project

5. Processes ensuring timely financial and output /results reporting and collaborative problem-solving are established and followed

Project management is ultimately about setting up and overseeing processes that get the work done. If a process isn't functioning effectively (it costs too much, results are substandard, accountability has been lost, participants are hoarding information, etc.) then it is reworked on the fly: *fail often, fail fast, and keep close to the customers/workers/output.*

The fundamental process of project management is managing

adaptability. As you may recall from Section Two, Darwin identified the ability to adapt as the core strength: *"It is not the strongest of the species that survives, or the most intelligent, but the ones most adaptable to change."*

In this sense, *project management is the process of managing cooperation, innovation and risk,* three key features of adaptability.

In the lexicon of management, this process of failing fast and failing often at a small enough scale to optimize problem-solving, transparency and accountability is called *agile development.* Our goal in learning project management is to learn how to optimize agile development, i.e. effective adaptability.

U.S. Air Force Colonel John Boyd developed a process to improve decision-making called the OODA loop (for observe, orient, decide, and act). In Boyd's system, decision-making results from a recurring cycle of observe-orient-decide-act in which feedback from previous decisions, new information and unfolding circumstances is incorporated in the next cycle of orientation, decision and action. This dynamic process epitomizes effective adaptation.

There are many resources for learning more about project management and virtually every organization offers fertile ground for practicing what you learn about managing *cooperation, innovation and risk.*

Your first and most important project is to manage and optimize your own learning and the accreditation of your skills, values and experience in creating value and solving problems.

Project management can be summarized by this quote from the Taoist sage Lao Tzu: *"If you do not change direction, you may end up where you are heading."*

Section Four: Higher Education Has Failed Students and the Economy

"I got a college degree, but now how do I get a job?" That's a common question, and it reflects the reality that a college degree no longer guarantees a job in today's economy. There are two basic reasons for this. The first is supply and demand: tens of millions of people have degrees now, and the supply of college graduates greatly exceeds the number of employers hiring workers on the basis of their college diploma.

The other reason is that Higher Education isn't preparing students to earn a livelihood in today's economy. This failing is systemic, meaning that it results from the structure of the system itself, rather than from defects in specific policies or programs.

The reality is the current system of Higher Education is broken and incapable of fixing itself. It has failed its most basic purpose, which is preparing students to earn a livelihood, and it depends on soaring student debt for funding. This is a double-whammy failure: Higher Education is burdening generations of students and their families with crippling debt while its product, a college diploma, has diminishing value in today's economy. A college diploma once guaranteed higher earnings and greater opportunity, but that is no longer true.

While the cost of college tuition has soared over 1,000% in a generation, a majority of recent college graduates are either jobless or working at jobs that do not require a college diploma; 53% of recent college graduates under the age of 25 are unemployed or doing work they could have done without going to college.

Student loans now exceed $1 trillion, with Federal loans ballooning from $115 billion to over $700 billion in a few short years. Only 37% of freshmen at four-year colleges graduate in four years and a mere 58% finally graduate in six years.

Defenders of Higher Education blame the economy for this poor showing but Higher Education is directly responsible for its failure to prepare graduates to earn a livelihood. A recent national study, *Academically Adrift*, found that over one third of college students "did not demonstrate any significant improvements in learning" critical thinking and other skills central to success in today's economy.

The study revealed that the measurable benefits of college are marginal for the majority of students. Given these structural flaws, it is no surprise that Higher Education is disconnected from the economy at the most fundamental level.

Google is widely viewed as a bellwether of the new economy. It is noteworthy, then, that Google has found that academic success has little correlation with being productive in the workplace. Lazlo Bock, senior vice president of people operations at Google, made the following comments in an interview published by the *New York Times* in June 2013:

"One of the things we've seen from all our data crunching is that G.P.A.'s (grade point averages) are worthless as a criteria for hiring, and test scores are worthless. Google famously used to ask everyone for a transcript and G.P.A.'s and test scores, but we don't anymore.... We found that they don't predict anything.

What's interesting is the proportion of people without any college education at Google has increased over time as well. So we have teams where you have 14 percent of the team made up of people who've never gone to college."

Doing well in college—earning high test scores and grades—has no measurable correlation with becoming an effective worker or manager. This is incontrovertible evidence that the entire Higher Education system is detached from the real economy: excelling in higher education has little discernible correlation to real-world skills or performance.

What is striking about these runaway costs and failure to prepare students for today's economy is the stunning lack of accountability: the Higher Education system continues to maintain it is cost-effective and successful even as evidence piles up that it is unaffordable and obsolete.

This lack of accountability and runaway pricing are hallmarks of a *cartel*, a quasi-monopoly that offers an illusory veneer of competition to mask its cartel nature. In the present system, colleges maintain a government-granted monopoly on accreditation: if you want a college degree, you have to pay the cartel its price, regardless of the education's quality or value. There is no accountability for the poor product because students have nowhere else to go for a diploma but the cartel.

Over 25% of students at major state colleges are already taking classes online, courses which are almost free to deliver as they require no classroom, campus or live instructor. In a competitive, accountable system, we would expect these savings to be passed onto students. Instead, tuition and fees continue rising every year, often at double-digit rates.

This double-whammy of ever-higher costs and declining value for the product (a college degree) creates a no-win dilemma for today's college-age students and millions of older workers who hope that going back to college will benefit their careers: the current system has demonstrably failed, but there are no alternatives except to forego a college diploma and hope that this won't damage one's career prospects.

We can summarize the failure of secondary and higher education in two key points:

> 1. The education system prepares students to advance to the next level of higher education, not to create value and profitably solve problems in the real economy.
>
> 2. The goal of the education system is for students to obtain a credential rather than skills that are essential in the real economy. The credential is seen as a proxy for knowledge or even wisdom; but a proxy of knowledge is not the same as knowledge embedded in human and social capital.

The credentials of higher education are thus largely worthless in the real economy, as proxies don't create value or solve problems; the emerging economy needs workers with practical skills and professionalism.

The next section lays out a practical path between the dead-end choices of a high-cost, low-value college diploma and not pursuing any accreditation: it's called *accredit yourself.*

This practical path combines one old idea, one new idea, one largely forgotten idea and one key insight into today's economy.

The old idea is *networking.* The advent of social-media networks has made this old idea new to some, but the idea that the best way to get a job is to network has been around for a long time.

This book will explain how to network effectively. Everything that people refer to as networking is not of equal value; much of what passes for networking has little value in terms of learning new skills and finding a job.

The new idea is *accredit yourself.* I will have much more to say about this, but one key piece is another old idea: *mastery.*

The largely forgotten idea is the essential role of *personal values* in creating *economic value,* either as an employee or in your own business. I have distilled these down into the eight essential skills of professionalism described in the previous section.

The person every employer wants is one who can learn whatever needs to be learned and solve problems with integrity, accountability, diligence, and do so while working effectively and easily with others.

The person who knows how to master new skills and apply them effectively with integrity, accountability and diligence will be able to get the job done, regardless of their major in college or the number of diplomas they earned. Indeed, as we have noted, college diplomas have little correlation to being effective on the job.

For those pursuing certain careers, a college diploma is still a requirement. We will discuss ways to lower the cost of obtaining that degree so that a lifetime of debt (student loans) can be avoided.

One key component of this path is to start seeking to *accredit yourself* on Day One of college, rather than waiting until Graduation Day to start preparing yourself to get a job.

In the conventional Higher Education timeline, the college student spends four to six years in an extension of adolescence, devoting himself to coursework and "the college experience" while working a few hours on campus or in a low-skill service job off campus. After four or five years of attending classes and investing tens of thousands of dollars in tuition, fees, books, room and board, etc., the student exits the Higher Education system with a diploma and then starts the process of finding a job in his chosen field.

From the perspective of *accrediting yourself,* this student just wasted four years: everything that he starts doing after graduation could have been done on Day One of his college experience.

In other words, college is not the goal; it is only one aspect of accrediting yourself. For some, college will be unnecessary, as a diploma won't serve to accredit their skills in their chosen field; for others, multiple degrees will be necessary (for example, physicians), and for those in neither category, higher education must be viewed as one part of accrediting yourself.

The key insight into today's economy is the *matrix of work* described in Section Two. Understanding this matrix is the key to choosing how you will accredit yourself.

Although you may be itching to learn more about accrediting yourself, it's important to first understand why the Higher Education system is obsolete.

The Old System: Systemic Scarcity of Media and Knowledge

We need to start with the historical roots of the current system, which arose from a profound scarcity of knowledge and instruction. In the ancient world, storing information was extremely expensive. Even after Gutenberg's printing press made mass-produced books available, books remained expensive; only a wealthy household could afford to buy more than a few books.

Instruction was similarly limited. Instruction in universities was often one person reading a text aloud to a classroom of students; this is the source of Cambridge University's longstanding academic rank of *Reader*.

The scarcity and high cost of written media led to the primacy of the oral lecture, as the only way to share knowledge was to concentrate students in one small geographic area to hear these lectures.

Despite the ubiquity of relatively inexpensive books, higher education in the 20th century remained essentially unchanged from the medieval model of students gathering to hear lectures drawn from large libraries. This high-cost structure insured that universities were elite institutions, finishing schools for the upper-class and a narrow channel of meritocracy for the best and brightest of the lower classes. In 1940, only 5% of adults had a college diploma.

World War II and the Advent of the Factory Model

The advent of global war in 1941required a rapid expansion of industry and managerial skills on an unprecedented scale. Unlike previous wars, oil, technology, industrial production, advanced research and management of these complex systems became paramount in World War II, and in response the Federal government ramped up the nation's small elitist system of higher education into a vast factory of universities and colleges producing millions of educated workers to serve the emerging knowledge-based economy.

This Factory Model was based on the principles of mass production:

college students attended the same lectures as hundreds of others and studied the same textbooks as thousands of others. The system of accrediting each college created an illusion of parity between institutions: while an Ivy League diploma was recognized as worth more than a standard-issue diploma, any bachelor's degree was deemed adequate proof of academic achievement.

This Factory Model yielded a three-part system: the traditional elite of academia, research and the professional schools (i.e. graduate and doctoral programs), mass-produced four-year bachelor's degrees, and a two-year community college system that served two roles: as preparation for a bachelor's degree and as a vocational school.

The need for white-collar managerial workers exceeded the output of college graduates in the 1950s and 60s, so the fundamentals of supply and demand favored college graduates, who found good-paying jobs relatively quickly and opportunities for advancement relatively expansive.

Colleges expanded quickly, using Federal and state funds to construct sprawling campuses. Costs were held down by modest salaries and benefits for non-tenured instructors and flat management structures.

In effect, a hodge-podge system tossed together in a national crisis became institutionalized. This is best revealed by this question: if we could start from scratch now, how would we design a cost-effective, responsive, accountable system of higher education?

Answers vary, but it certainly wouldn't resemble today's failing, costly, obsolete system.

The Higher Education Cartel

The basic structure of Higher Education can be summarized in eight points:

1.	As noted above, higher education is a legacy system based on the scarcity of recorded knowledge (printed and other media) and lectures. Both recorded knowledge and lectures are now essentially free and readily available to everyone with a digital device.

2.	The current higher education model is a factory composed of lectures and mass-distributed coursework/tests. The student moves down the assembly line, attending the same lectures as other students, reading the same materials and taking the same tests.

When the student receives a passing grade in a quasi-arbitrary number of courses, he or she is accredited, i.e. issued a diploma.

3.   In terms of its financial structure, higher education is a cartel-like system that limits its product (accredited instruction) and restricts its output (credentials, diplomas). This creates an *artificial scarcity*.

4.   The cartel's basic mechanism of maintaining non-competitive pricing is to enforce an *artificial scarcity of credentials*. The cartel's control of a product that is in high demand (college diplomas) frees it from outside competition and free-market price discovery, enabling it to charge customers (students) an extraordinary premium for a product whose value is entirely scarcity-based.

This is the very definition of a *rent-seeking cartel*, a cartel that extracts premiums solely on the basis of an artificial scarcity. By their very nature, rent-seeking cartels are exploitive and parasitic, drawing resources from those who can least afford to pay high premiums and misallocating capital that could have been invested in productive social investments. The term *rents* in this context means that the cartel collects a premium without providing any corresponding additional value.

Since the higher education cartel is the sole provider of accreditation (college diplomas), it is unaccountable for its failure to prepare its customers (students) for productive employment in the emerging economy. If a diploma is portrayed as essential, students must pay the cartel even if the cartel's product is ineffective and obsolete.

5.   The four-year college system is profoundly disconnected from the economy. That the cartel's product has little practical application is not considered a factor in the value of the product (diploma), a *credential that is a proxy for knowledge rather than proof of practical knowledge.*

6.   The present system of higher education is unaffordable for all but the wealthy. The cartel's solution to its high prices, $1 trillion in student loan debt, is a crushing burden on both individuals and society at large.

7.   The higher education cartel is an intrinsically elitist force, as its survival as a rent-seeking cartel is based on limiting what is now essentially free: knowledge and instruction. In other words, the higher education cartel charges an extraordinary premium for a free product.

8.   The only way the Higher Education cartel can continue to charge a premium for nearly-free products is to actively *mystify its product* (by attributing secular sanctity to its diplomas) and *promote an artificial value for this product using public relations and political lobbying*. In other words, the higher education cartel operates on the same principles as other parasitic cartels: it depends on the government to enforce the scarcity of its product, and it uses public relations to mask its cartel structure and systemic failure to fulfill its stated purpose.

Charging a Premium for Elitist Social Connections: The Spoils System

It has long been understood that the value proposition in attending an elite university is not the instruction but the social connections forged with children of the Elite, influential professors and alumni. This can be summarized by the expression, "it's who you know, not what you know." The unspoken assumption is that a great many people are equally qualified for lucrative positions in finance and governance, and the selection process is based less on talent and creativity than on being socially connected to those with the power to hire or introduce candidates to other influential people.

As the number of qualified candidates for these relatively few positions rises, the premium elite universities can charge for social access to the wealthy and influential also rises. As online essayist Michael O. Church has explained, this is actually a pernicious consequence of a system that is rotting from within. The rising importance of Elitist social connections reflects a system that is increasingly a spoils system based on who you know rather than merit. This spoils system is characteristic of sclerotic kleptocracies that are eventually destabilized by rising income disparity and the economic stagnation that results from the erosion of meritocracy-based social mobility.

The rising value of Elitist social connections reflects a system in which opportunity is diminishing—a system that is getting poorer, not wealthier.

The recognition that social connections mean more than merit, hard work, creativity or talent fuels parents' desperation to get their children into elite universities. But since an increasing number of others are playing the same manic game of getting their kids into the "right" kindergarten or prep school, enrichment activities, test-preparation program, etc., this pathway leaves more disappointed parents and students ill-prepared for earning a livelihood outside the privileged spoils-system.

This system enables ever-higher prices for access to elite universities while the purported value of the access declines as an ever-larger number of graduates seek the same few slots in the spoils system.

Pursuing acceptance to an elite university with the goal of securing a slot in the spoils system is guaranteed to disappoint the vast majority of students and their parents, as the number of slots in the various Elite institutions is so much smaller than the number of qualified candidates.

Approaching Higher Education with the goal of acquiring mastery of productive knowledge and the eight essential skills is the higher-value path. This is the essence of *accredit yourself.*

The Economy Changed; the Factory Model Didn't

The U.S. economy has changed in fundamental ways since the heyday of the Factory Model of Higher Education in the 1950s and 60s. In that era, the U.S. maintained a near-monopoly on capital and industry as war-ravaged Europe and Japan were still rebuilding their shattered economies. The rapid expansion of the consumer economy demanded an equally rapid expansion in the white-collar workforce of managers and marketers, and those with college diplomas were a scarce commodity who could command a premium on the labor market. Healthcare was cheap and economic growth robust; overhead costs were low and it behooved companies to offer stable employment, low-cost benefits and pension plans.

The system had another important feature: it was assumed that employers would provide new college graduates on-the-job training to prepare them for productive work. A college diploma was evidence of the student's perseverance and ability to navigate institutional processes, not his readiness to produce value in the real-world economy. A college degree was a stamp on what I term the *higher education passport* that enabled the holder to enter the white-collar workforce: the *higher education passport is a proxy for knowledge rather than proof of knowledge.* The school or subject was less important than the accreditation (diploma) itself.

These employer-operated training programs were often lengthy and comprehensive; in effect, employers shouldered the enormously expensive task of transforming a green college graduate with little to no actual job-related skills into a productive employee.

The 1970s upended many aspects of this high-growth era. Energy crises bled the economy of efficiency and purchasing power, and the era of high wages for low-skill factory work gave way to the first waves of global competition, automation, computerization and robotics.

This structural shift from industrial to post-industrial employment fueled a systemic need for workers with advanced knowledge of computers, software and related technical skills, as well as a secondary pool of workers able to deploy these new technologies in every sector of the economy: defense, design, communications, marketing, human resources, government, finance, engineering, etc.

The Factory Model could adjust to this new need by expanding curricula in these new fields while keeping the traditional departments and schools on a continued expansionary track.

Demographics played a role as well; the 60+ million Baby Boom that had begun entering college in the mid-60s reached its college-age apogee in the 1970s.

This legacy system of mass-produced college diplomas made the transition from an industrial economy to a post-industrial economy because tens of millions of college graduates were absorbed into four expanding sectors: the financialization industry (the so-called FIRE economy of finance, insurance and real estate), the consumer-driven sectors of sales and marketing, the government funded fields of healthcare and education and the digital technology industries.

Those with advanced degrees found high-level jobs within academia itself, government or industry.

All of these industries have reached the point of saturation and diminishing returns: financialization has hollowed out the economy and triggered systemic instability; sales and marketing are being revolutionized by digital technologies; the enormous resources being poured into healthcare and education feed vested interests while yielding fewer measurable results, and the digital technologies are automating not just engineering and management in every sector but the very process of engineering advances.

Costly on-the-job training programs have vanished as enterprises are too stretched to invest time and capital in training new employees, knowing that competitors may well poach them once their training is complete. Employers in today's economy want employees who can start working productively on Day One, not six months from now after extensive training. In today's era of global competition, lavishing months of costly training on domestic workers makes no financial sense when lower-cost employees with job-ready skills can be hired by the corporation's overseas operations.

The Factory Model of higher education has failed to make the transition to the emerging economy, and indeed, cannot make the transition as it is structurally disconnected from today's economy.

Degree Inflation and the False Promise of Specialization

Not only does a general education no longer prepare students for work in the new economy: there is no longer an insatiable need for ever greater numbers of advanced degree specialists and PhDs in every field.

Many PhDs have been reduced to what I call *academic ronin*, highly educated teachers or researchers who cannot get a permanent tenured position within academia as the number of qualified candidates far exceeds the number of jobs. It is not uncommon to find hundreds of PhDs applying for one tenure-track position. As with all fields in today's economy, the competition is global. This imbalance between the huge number of people with advanced degrees and the small number of secure positions leaves the majority with few choices other than an insecure career of wandering from institution to institution on short-term contracts—hence the reference to masterless samurai in feudal Japan (*ronin*).

The widely held assumption that advanced degrees in STEM fields (science, technology, engineering, mathematics) are a ticket to a lucrative, secure job is also being upended. A 2013 study of National Science Foundation data on born-in-the-U.S.A. PhD graduates in science and engineering found that two-thirds were either still job hunting or languishing in a temporary postdoctoral position as a low-paid research assistant.

This same structural imbalance between the rising number of highly educated jobseekers and a stagnating number of positions requiring their level of education is also visible in the professions: law, architecture, MBAs, etc. Media accounts of attorneys losing jobs that paid $170,000 and after a lengthy job search eventually landing a $40,000-per-year position are increasingly common.

The Higher Education system consistently overpromises and under-delivers on real-world results. The gap between its rosy public-relations claims and the experiences of graduates has widened to the point that the system's PR has lost credibility to those who examine the post-graduation jobs data.

Higher Education's self-serving solution to the widening disconnect between the promised benefits of additional degrees and the stark reality of today's job market has been to over-promise the benefits of ever more specialized degrees. Where a degree in Marketing was once sufficient, now there are Master's Programs in Pharmaceutical Marketing. Management degrees (the ubiquitous Masters of Business Administration) are now subdividing into Casino Management, and so on.

This trend exemplifies the profound disconnect between Higher Education and the emerging economy: as Higher Education narrows its focus on increasingly specific jobs, the economy is blurring the lines between such narrow categories of jobs and creatively destroying or reworking entire industries. Rather than demanding more specialized knowledge of siloed jobs, the economy is demanding collaborative work across multiple fields and disciplines. The more specialized the education, the more likely it will be outdated, bypassed or undervalued by a dynamic economy that increasingly depends on cross-fertilization and collaboratively developed projects, knowledge bases and skills.

In effect, Higher Education is predicting what jobs will be in demand (or still exist) five, ten and twenty years in the future by promoting specialized degrees. Is there any evidence that Higher Education has the tools to accurately predict what jobs will be in demand in the future?

This increasing specialization of degrees simply gives Human Resources departments a perfect reason to reject job seekers: sorry, your degree is in casino management, we need someone who can manage software implementation.

If you wanted to doom students to economic dead-ends, you'd funnel them into narrow, specialized degrees—exactly what the Higher Education system is doing.

Legacy systems fail for a number of reasons, including loss of adaptability, higher costs coupled with diminishing returns, institutional sclerosis, vested interests incapable of reforming themselves out of a job, mission creep, loss of the original purpose, and so on. But the deeper reason is that the legacy system itself is the impediment to progress; as a result, even modest reforms trigger collapse of a system that has become obsolete.

The economy of the 2010s is undergoing a change just as dramatic and wrenching as the transition from industrial to post-industrial. The economy —and competition for capital, skills, goods and services—is global. Overhead costs such as healthcare have soared, making hiring workers an expensive proposition. With roughly 40% of the workforce holding a college diploma, the scarcity of college-educated workers has been replaced by a surplus of workers with university degrees.

Granting more advanced degrees does not magically create positions for those holding freshly issued diplomas. Instead, degree inflation is at work: what once required a high school diploma now requires a bachelor's degree, what once required a bachelor's degree now requires a Master's degree, and so on.

As corporate and government Human Resource departments have increasingly fenced off even low-level jobs as requiring a college diploma, a bachelor's degree is becoming the entry-level minimum, replacing the high school diploma. Further up the food chain, Masters Degrees are also in surplus, pushing many ambitious youth into PhD programs, in the hope that a PhD will guarantee a high-paying job. Alas, as noted above, there is a growing surplus of people with PhDs. Some claim the unemployment rate for PhDs is very low, but these surveys do not measure under-employment, i.e. did the PhD take a position that only required a lesser degree?

The Higher Education cartel is perfectly happy to encourage degree inflation (at enormous expense to students, of course), but this zeal for issuing student-loan funded diplomas fails to address two structural disparities: the gap between the skills needed to prosper in the emerging economy and the skills colleges are providing students, and the widening income/wealth/education gap between the wealthy and the non-wealthy.

As higher education costs soar, the divide between wealthy and poor families widens as non-wealthy students are forced to become debt-serfs to pay for college. A system that forces poor households to shoulder student loans for decades in return for marginal-utility college degrees is not just immoral, it is recklessly predatory. Yet this is the system Higher Education supports and defends.

There is a profound disconnect between the Higher Education cartel and what higher education should cost in a world where information, instruction and knowledge have fallen to the cost of bandwidth, i.e. near-zero. What was once costly and scarce (knowledge and instruction) is now nearly free and abundant, readily available on any digital device anywhere in the world with a connection to the Web. There is no need to concentrate students in a campus with a library; every web-connected digital device is a library and university combined.

In essence, the foundation of higher education has been completely upended: knowledge and instruction, once costly and scarce, are now abundant and nearly free. The only pricing power left to Higher Education cartel is the *artificial scarcity* of credentials.

That is not the power of a productive system; it is the power of a parasitic, predatory system.

A Credential/Degree Does Not Verify Mastery

Let's start by listing what various forms of accreditation actually verify.

A diploma issued by a professional school (nursing, architecture, law, etc.) is presumed to prepare the graduate to pass the licensing exam that enables them to practice in their field. This is a model that functions because the goal is to prepare the student for an objective appraisal of their knowledge, and there is a feedback loop: schools whose graduates fail the licensing exam in great numbers will eventually lose students based on their poor performance.

Unfortunately, this model of objective testing of graduates' knowledge and feedback for poor performance by the college is limited to professional schools. In my view, this model should be extended to the entire higher education system. This professional system of verification and feedback is the foundation of the *Nearly Free University* model.

A non-professional-school four-year bachelor's degree verifies that the student completed the requirements of the minimum number of courses to graduate. The diploma does not verify the knowledge the student learned or the critical skills he acquired, if any, in the coursework, nor does it verify the student learned how to learn, that is, that he has the ability to be his own teacher.

The degree does nothing to verify that the student has the requisite core values needed for gainful employment, for example integrity, professionalism and accountability. *The higher education credential is a proxy for knowledge rather than proof of practical knowledge.*

Given the wide spectrum of quality in college coursework, a bachelor's degree offers essentially no useful verification of skills, values or knowledge. The only trait that a bachelor's degree verifies is the student's ability to navigate (or game) an institution of Higher Education long enough and successfully enough to gather the minimum number of credits for graduation.

Credentials prepare students not to create value in the real economy but for acceptance to the next level in the accreditation bureaucracy.

A Master's Degree offers an equivalent dearth of useful verification; if the Master's Program required a thesis, the graduate's thesis offers some evidence of the student's ability to write clearly and succinctly (assuming the thesis is solely the student's work, something that is difficult to verify in an age of copy-and-paste and academic ghostwriters).

A doctorate (PhD) verifies the graduate's knowledge of the field and their ability to perform independent research. The PhD degree does not verify the graduate's teaching ability or any other soft skill, or their professionalism and values, though some of these traits may be visible to the graduate's faculty advisors. But the PhD itself does not verify anything but the graduate's knowledge and research/written communication capabilities.

In professions such as architecture and law, a diploma is not enough in most states to begin practicing in the real world; graduates are required to pass a test that verifies their knowledge of the profession's essentials.

These professional exams verify the graduate's basic body of knowledge, but do not verify the graduate's values, ability to work effectively with others, or their general competence in the actual practice of their profession.

The only way to verify working knowledge and professionalism is to provide a multi-year supervised apprenticeship of on-the-job training. Trade union apprenticeships are a traditional example of multiyear on-the-job training programs, as are residency programs for doctors and nurses.

Physicians must actually practice their profession under the supervision of experienced physicians in a multi-year residency program before they are licensed to practice medicine. This long training and apprenticeship verifies not just their knowledge and experience but also offers an opportunity to verify their values and soft skills of communication, collaboration with others, etc.

In the armed forces, soldiers, sailors and marines must verify their knowledge and professional abilities on active duty to advance in rank.

This brief overview reveals just how little useful information about a graduate is verified by a college degree--even an advanced degree. Obtaining a credential can be gamed, gaining practical knowledge and professionalism cannot. A proxy of knowledge and skills is not the same as practical knowledge and skills or professionalism. This is core failure of the higher education cartel.

Given that the ideal job candidate, regardless of the field or position, has learned how to master new knowledge quickly and applies high professional values and standards to every task, we can see just how low-value a college degree is in terms of assessing and selecting employees.

Since a college degree only verifies the graduate's ability to navigate a Higher Education institution, the task of verifying everything of importance and value to employers, customers and colleagues falls to the student. This is why it's essential to acquire the eight essential soft skills that create economic value and to learn how to *accredit yourself*.

The Nearly Free University Model

My book *The Nearly Free University and the Emerging Economy: The Revolution in Higher Education* offers a template for a system of higher education that is an integral part of the emerging economy and that is extremely low in cost. In The *Nearly Free University* model, students earn credentials by passing exams that demonstrate their grasp of knowledge—the method of demonstrating knowledge in professions such as medicine, architecture and law.

Though the formal *Nearly Free University* does not yet exist, all the pieces are already in place. The opportunity to learn and accredit your own knowledge and experience are available to everyone with an Internet connection and a digital device.

To understand the process of accrediting yourself, let's briefly review how the *Nearly Free University model* works.

There are four broad technology-enabled solutions that can free higher education from its current cartel limitations:

1.		*Accredit the student, not the school.* By accrediting the student rather than the institution, we remove control of the credential supply and pricing from the cartel and establish the value of what the student has mastered by objective standards.

The concept of accrediting the student, not the school is well-established in the professions. Obtaining a law or architecture degree does not confer the right to practice those professions in the real world; one must demonstrate mastery of the field by passing a lengthy examination.

How difficult would it be to transfer this concept to all students in higher education? In the digital age, there is no technological or cost barrier to establishing a largely automated online procedure for taking exams and making the results available to prospective employers or collaborators.

2.		*Structure learning such that it no longer depends on large physical campuses and costly administration.* Higher education has two claims of value: one, the issuance of credentials (diplomas), and two, the claim that the product (instruction) can only be gained in a classroom managed by a high-cost bureaucracy.

In the digital age, learning is no longer tethered to large physical campuses and expensive administration. Anyone with an Internet connection and a digital device has access to essentially unlimited knowledge, lessons and tutorials.

3.		*Tailor the curriculum to the needs of the real-world emerging economy and the methods of learning to the individual student.*

The value proposition in education is no longer the live lecturer who assigns the same material to hundreds of students or the administration of the factory model of education; it is the *assembly of nearly-free learning tools* that fit the needs of the real emerging economy and the individual student. Classes no longer need be scheduled and attended during working hours; digital courses are available 24 hours a day, 7 days a week year-round.

4. *Eliminate the artificial scarcity of admissions and accreditation.* The Nearly Free University model eliminates this artificial scarcity and the Elite-controlled spoils system it creates. The Nearly Free University is open to all; it has no artificial scarcity, no spoils system and no Elites.

Not Just Cheaper, but Better

There are three key technologies in the Nearly Free University model:

1. *Digital media.* Everything that can be digitized is nearly free to distribute

2. *Adaptive learning,* where software tailors curricula, lessons and methods to each individual student

3. *Massively networked participants*

The nearly-free cost of digital media is self-explanatory; what needs to be mentioned is the extraordinary willingness of people to share their knowledge —not just via massively open online courses (MOOCs) from enterprises such as the Khan Academy, Coursera or Saylor.com, but from what I term the *University of YouTube.* This vast library of lessons is expanding daily, and includes instruction on everything from sewing a button to digital logic design.

We are enjoying what my colleague Mark Gallmeier terms *the age of unlimited pedagogy,* yet our institutions are essentially unchanged from 60 years ago.

That each person has a unique set of propensities, talents and preferred ways of learning is self-evident; the ability to tailor instruction to each individual is the promise of adaptive learning tools, which include a wider range of methods and curricula than the Factory Model can possibly manage.

Adaptive learning is not just a cheaper way of learning—it is clearly a better way of learning. As Salman Khan, founder of the Khan Academy, recently observed, "Students can progress at their own pace and continue to prove their knowledge long after the formal course is over." This is but one example of the benefits of adaptive learning.

The core of adaptive learning can be summarized by Nobel laureate Herbert Simon's observation: *"Learning results from what the student does and thinks and only from what the student does and thinks."*

Massively Networked Participants Fuel Innovation

It's not just the coursework that is open to everyone—the entire spectrum of data, experimental results, critiques and "What worked, what didn't" is available to every participant in the Nearly Free University model.

This leverages a central tenet of network theory, what sociologist Mark Granovetter described as *"the strength of weak ties."* The most efficient networks are those that link to the broadest range of information, knowledge, and experience. Narrow expertise actually limits problem-solving.

Network theory also informs the key concept: *accredit yourself.* We are already accustomed to accrediting restaurants, hotels and a host of other services via user reviews; the Web offers the possibility of assembling one's own accreditation from trustworthy sources whose own credibility can also be verified by the *strength of weak ties.*

This concept also explains why some types of networking are far more successful than others. We'll discuss both of these applications in more detail later.

Should I Get a College Degree?

The stark reality that the value of college diplomas is declining raises pressing and difficult-to-answer questions for young people: should I get a college degree? If I don't have a college degree, how will a get a career/job?

It raises similar questions of older workers: should I go back to school to earn another degree?

To answer these questions, we need to break them down into smaller inquiries.

> 1. Do you want to enter a profession that requires a degree and a licensing certification, such as medicine, law or architecture, or a trade that requires a two-year certificate and a licensing certification?

These questions are impossible to answer without directly experiencing the field first-hand. If you think you might enjoy being a nurse or physician, then volunteer in a hospital for a summer. If you think you might enjoy being an attorney, then volunteer for a summer in a law office. There is no substitute for experiencing the day-to-day routines and tasks of whatever profession interests you.

Thinking you might like a field is not the same as knowing you like the field based on months of hands-on experience. Many people who reckoned they'd like practicing law and who earn a law degree without ever having worked in a real-world law firm discover to their surprise they dislike the actual practice of law.

Thinking you will enjoy the salary and status of a job is not the same as actually enjoying the day-to-day practice of the job.

After spending a few months working in your field of interest—a hospital, law office, architecture firm, restaurant kitchen, farm, kindergarten classroom, bakery, auto body shop, graphic design firm, pharmacy, biotech lab, social services office, etc. —you will know if that's the sort of work you want to do for years or decades. You may well discover if it's a good fit for you within the first few days.

2.   Is there an oversupply of qualified people in this field?

This question matters because the last thing you want is to devote years of your life and tens of thousands of dollars for a credential or license that is in oversupply, i.e. the number of qualified people far exceeds the number of job openings in the field.

Supply and demand are in constant flux. As demand for specific skills rises in a stagnating economy, more people seek the training as a way of insuring a secure job. If enough people flood into the field, the number of qualified people eventually exceeds the number of jobs.

This reality forces every student to look into a crystal ball and predict what the job market will look like in their chosen field four, five and ten years down the road.

Though this may seem impossible to do, talking to people in the field and in the training programs will enable you to make an informed assessment.

Many professions that once absorbed all graduates such as law are now oversupplied with qualified applicants. As degree inflation has become the norm, fields in which as master's degree once practically guaranteed a job are now plagued by an oversupply of people with master's degrees. Even a doctorate (PhD) is no longer a guarantee, as many PhDs are underemployed or working as *academic ronin* in insecure positions.

> 3. Do you want to work for large-scale organizations such as a corporation or state agency with bureaucratic human resources departments that see college degrees as passport stamps, i.e. the minimum level of credentialing needed to even apply for a job?

If so, then you will need that passport stamp. Your challenge then becomes 1) doing so without going into debt and 2) structuring your college years around gaining the eight essential skills and accrediting yourself so you're actually prepared to create value and profitably solve problems when you exit college.

The only way to go to college without going into debt is to either obtain a full scholarship, a benefit that is increasingly rare, or attend a state university while living at home or with a relative and working part-time.

Having a part-time job is not a detriment, it is an enormous asset, as a part-time job in your field of interest will give you invaluable experience to learn, build networks and accredit yourself.

If paying work for beginners in your chosen field is scarce, the next best thing is to work for someone with the skills and social capital to mentor you and provide opportunities that are only available to those within his/her professional network. Such work could be unrelated to your field of interest; as we saw in Section One, those with social capital and the willingness to learn can acquire hard skills.

> 4. Does your field of interest offer jobs in small enterprises without human resources departments, i.e. *do-ocracy* enterprises where what you can do matters more than what proxy of knowledge (diploma) you have?

A great many jobs can be learned and mastered without formal diploma programs. Small enterprises are by necessity *do-ocracies*, where the more you do the more influence and earnings you gain, as there is not enough money lying around to pay under-performers, whether they have a degree or not.

This was the point made by Google's vice-president earlier in this section: being able to perform at a high professional level, creating value and solving problems, is what every enterprise wants and needs, and the more advanced enterprises have realized that a proxy for knowledge (a degree) does not necessarily mean the graduate has the hard and soft skills to create value and solve problems.

How many worker-owned co-ops require a college degree of all their workers? Once your livelihood depends on the productivity and professionalism of your colleagues, the value of a degree pales to near-zero compared to what the person can accomplish with their human and social capital.

Self-employed people who work within a network of other professionals do not need a college degree to get hired; they hired themselves. (Licensed professionals such as certified public accountants will of course need whatever credentials are required to take their professional licensing exam.)

The point here is that a degree doesn't guarantee there will be a job for every graduate, and that not having a degree doesn't preclude having a successful and fulfilling career. Those who want to become licensed professionals will have to complete the professional training. Those who want to work in large-scale corporations and state agencies with bureaucratic human resources departments may be expected to have a degree of some sort just to apply for a position.

But these highly bureaucratic organizations are precisely the ones most likely to be disrupted going forward, because the gains to be reaped by replacing their inefficiencies are the lowest hanging fruit.

A relatively few professions (such as physicians) are guaranteed jobs by dint of certification and licensing. For the vast majority of workers, establishing as livelihood may or may not require a college degree or licensing, but it will certainly require the professionalism and skills required to work productively in *do-ocracies*.

Rather than ask, should I go to college or not?, the more insightful question is, what do I need to do to prepare myself to create value and profitably solve problems in *do-ocracies* within my selected field?

Summary: Putting the Nearly Free University Model to Work for You

The Higher Education cartel promotes four fallacies that enable it to siphon hundreds of billions of dollars in revenues:

1.   That a proxy of knowledge (a diploma or credential) is equivalent to practical working knowledge and human capital; it is not.

2.   That the solution to the declining value of a bachelor's degree is getting additional degrees, i.e. degree inflation. But obtaining more proxies of knowledge does not prepare a student to create value and profitably solve problems in the real economy.

3.   That knowledge and skills acquired outside the Higher Education cartel are of little value because the cartel did not issue a proxy (credential) of that knowledge.

4.   That there is no need to teach the essential values and skills of professionalism; these are magically acquired by osmosis in Factory Model classrooms.

The claims of the Higher Education cartel are strikingly Orwellian, as each claim is the reversal of reality.

The cartel's proxies of knowledge (credentials) are intrinsically low-value because they do not objectively verify any actual acquisition of knowledge or skills.

Obtaining additional proxies of knowledge (at enormous expense) is equally low-value for the same reasons.

Knowledge acquired outside the cartel is not worthless—it is the foundation of the professionalism and practical skills that are valuable in the real economy.

Professionalism is not gained by osmosis or magic; it must be learned like any other skill.

While some professions still require degrees, the value of college diplomas outside these specific professions is declining because the diplomas do not actually verify the student acquired practical knowledge or skills.

It is thus up to each person who isn't in a licensed profession to accredit themselves by demonstrating objective, verifiable evidence of mastery and professionalism.

In *the age of unlimited pedagogy*, knowledge is essentially free. The process of acquiring economically useful mastery of a subject requires a structured curriculum, and the ideal structured curriculum is one designed to fit the aptitudes and learning preferences of each individual.

The tools to design such a curriculum for ourselves are available to anyone willing to do the work.

Just as learning is now untethered from the Higher Education cartel, accreditation is now available to everyone.

Section Five: Accrediting Yourself

The Need to Accredit Yourself

Let's take a moment to summarize our findings:

1.   The Higher Education system is a self-serving cartel that charges astronomical prices for its diminishing-value products (i.e. college diplomas) by enforcing an artificial scarcity of credentials in an era of essentially free knowledge.

2.   The Higher Education system does not recognize or teach the critical skills and core values of professionalism needed to secure a livelihood (get a job or start a business) in today's economy.

3.   College degrees do not verify the graduate's knowledge, skills, talents or core values. The goal within the current system is earning credentials, not actual knowledge/skills. A credential is not knowledge; it is a proxy with no verifiable value.

4.   An alternative system, The Nearly Free University, is emergent but not yet issuing credentials (accredited degrees).

This means it's up to each student to learn on their own what college doesn't provide: the eight essential skills/values of professionalism and the ability to create value and solve problems.

Since a college degree accredits essentially nothing about the student's professionalism, knowledge, skills or human capital, we must each accredit ourselves by demonstrating these attributes in the real world.

Fortunately, a vast spectrum of knowledge is available for free (or low cost) online, and many people are ready and willing to help you for free.

The Necessary Steps to Accrediting Yourself

The core of *accredit yourself* is summarized by Emerson's dictum: *Do the thing and you shall have the power.* In practical terms, accrediting yourself requires first acquiring the eight essential skills of professionalism and whatever hard skills are needed to be effective in your chosen field, and then verifying your mastery of the skills by completing projects that demonstrate your working knowledge, creativity, experience and ability to learn, solve problems and work with others. The next step is to assemble accounts from trustworthy colleagues, employers, advisors and peers with direct knowledge of your contributions that demonstrate your experience, abilities, skills and core values.

The last step is to share these credentials with networks of people, agencies and enterprises that are active in your chosen field.

One way to think about the process of accrediting yourself is to imagine that you're filling in all the blanks that are filled by professional verification processes such as residencies for doctors and nurses and apprenticeship programs for union tradespeople.

Put yourself in the shoes of an employer, client or customer: what would you need to know about a person before entrusting them with key tasks?

You'd want to know that they have demonstrated they can get the job done by completing similar projects. You'd want to know they've shown they can learn new material quickly, that they possess the emotional intelligence and maturity to respond positively to fair criticism, and that they've demonstrated the ability to collaborate effectively with others, both in person and online. You'd want to see evidence that they solved problems efficiently. You'd want trustworthy sources to confirm the candidate's personal integrity and professionalism.

Only when you've been able to verify all these attributes would you have the confidence to entrust this person with a job.

Put another way: the process of accrediting yourself lowers the risk of hiring you. If you put yourself in the shoes of an employer, you will quickly realize that hiring someone based on their resume/CV (curriculum vitae) is risky for a number of reasons.

One is that resumes can be inflated or exaggerated, and negative feedback from former employers has been left out. A resume is a sales pitch, not an objective report of the applicant's experience, character and skills. The applicant claims to have performed this task, but what actual evidence is there for that claim?

How can the prospective employer tell if an applicant is revealing his true character in a brief interview? We all know people can maintain a charming veneer that masks their real values, and that people will say whatever helps them get the job.

By accrediting your real-world projects in detail and providing verification from trustworthy sources, you will remove most of the risk from the hiring process.

Which applicant would you pick, all other qualifications being equal: the one with a resume full of unsupported claims and a few personal references of unknown trustworthiness, or the applicant with multiple projects detailing his skills and values and multiple sources that can be verified with basic online searches?

The first applicant is a high-risk hire, the second one is a low-risk hire because he's provided the prospective employer with a wealth of easily verifiable information about his skills, values and human and social capital.

We can summarize the process of accrediting yourself in five steps:

1.   Learn and put into daily practice the eight essential skills/values of professionalism

2.   Learn how to learn to mastery, i.e. master new knowledge and apply new skills.

3.   Demonstrate your mastery and problem-solving by completing real-world projects

4.   Assemble independently verifiable accounts of your abilities, experience, skills and professionalism from people with direct knowledge of your completed projects: colleagues, employers, supervisors, advisors, mentors, clients and peers.

5.   Distribute your completed projects and third-party verifications to networks of people, agencies and enterprises that are active in your chosen field.

Each of these steps may be daunting to individuals accustomed to the Factory Model of assigned coursework and passively following instructions, but there is no other pathway to securing a livelihood in today's economy. It is essential to acquire the habit of learning new material and applying new skills to real-world problem-solving, to demonstrate perseverance and professionalism even in difficult circumstances, and to learn how to collaborate effectively with others. This is the process of building human and social capital.

Potential employers and clients have no way to verify your talents, abilities, experience, skills and values except what you provide them. The graduate who will be in demand is the one who demonstrates he/she possesses the eight essential skills and has real-world experience in solving problems in a variety of settings.

The more people who know about your experience, skills and professionalism, the more likely it will be that someone will want to hire you or offer you an opportunity. Acquiring skills, demonstrating effectiveness, verifying one's abilities and professionalism and then distributing this information to appropriate networks—these are the essential steps to accrediting yourself.

Accrediting yourself doesn't just demonstrate your abilities to perform a specific task; being able to complete this multi-step process shows prospective employers and collaborators that you have everything it takes to help them accomplish their goals: grit, perseverance, integrity, good communications skills and professionalism. You will be demonstrating that you are the complete package, the real deal, the kind of person everyone wants to work with because you make working with you easy and make everyone you work with look good.

Let's examine each of the five steps in order.

The Processes of Professionalism

One of the key characteristics of accrediting yourself is that is a series of processes. Setting goals is important, but the real work is performed by establishing processes and habits that generate goal-oriented results: *we are what we do every day.*

For example, creativity isn't just the classic flash of inspiration or insight: it is a process of consistent experimentation, testing the results and developing the idea or dropping it and moving on to the next one, a process captured by the phrase *fail often, fail fast.*

Professionals are not born; they learn the values and acquire the habits of professionalism the same way we learn anything, with daily effort and practice directed by goals. We covered this process in Section Three, *Investing in Ourselves.*

The goal of professionalism guides every step of our learning, job search, career development and how we deal with challenge, failure and disappointment.

One practical way to understand professionalism is to ask: how does a professional deal with unemployment? The answer is that *the professional never considers himself unemployed*; he is self-employed at all times, building human and social capital. The professional response to unemployment is to be productive for eight hours a day, regardless of the pay or lack thereof, day in and day out, rain or shine, because work isn't just about earning money, it's about creating value and meaning and living authentically.

This requires self-discipline and the development of productive habits, i.e. investing in ourselves.

Let's review the eight essential skills of professionalism:

1. Learn challenging new material over one's entire productive life

2. Creatively apply newly-mastered knowledge and skills to a variety of fields

3. Be adaptable, responsible and accountable in all work environments

4. Apply a full spectrum of entrepreneurial skills to any task, i.e. take ownership of one's work

5. Work collaboratively and effectively with others, both in person and remotely

6. Communicate clearly and effectively in all work environments

7. Continually build human and social capital, i.e. knowledge and networks

8. Possess a practical working knowledge of financial records and project management

We've discussed various aspects of these skills in preceding sections, but now we will address key attributes of professionalism in greater depth. These include self-awareness and self-management, self-learning to mastery, maintaining motivation, building networks and becoming familiar with financial records and project management.

The key words in this section are *learning* and *processes*. Professionalism is lifelong learning and understanding that solving problems and creating value are the result of processes, not just ideas, inspiration, genius or goals. All of those play a part, but the work is done by processes. The higher we move up the value-creation/problem-solving chain, the more intuitive and flexible the processes tend to be. It's not so much what you know now; it's what you'll be learning today and tomorrow and applying to solving problems over the rest of your productive life.

Professionalism is valued in every field, white-collar and blue-collar, and in every person. Professionalism makes life and work easier, and problems easier to solve.

Self-Awareness/ Self-Knowledge and Self-Management/Self-Discipline

The surest way to waste time and money and derail any project is to deal exclusively with unprofessional people: people who overpromise but under-deliver, who don't show up on time, make excuses for their lack of effectiveness, blame others for their own shortcomings, throw a tantrum when their work is critiqued, routinely make offensive remarks, exhibit disruptive behavior, dump unaddressed mental health issues on colleagues, inject personal issues into the workplace—the list is nearly endless but the results are always the same: unprofessional conduct is toxic to productivity and effectiveness.

We are all beset with a variety of inner conflicts, emotions, weaknesses and challenges; this is the human condition. But to solve problems, create value and collaborate effectively with others, we need to learn to separate our personal issues from getting the work done. This is the foundation of professional conduct and courtesy, and it requires a self-awareness/self-knowledge that guides our self-management and self-discipline.

Acquiring self-awareness and developing self-management are the first essential steps in becoming professional. The process of accrediting yourself will open many opportunities to increase your self-awareness and practice self-discipline.

Why is self-knowledge so critical to success and personal happiness? There are two reasons: it takes self-knowledge to choose a career path that aligns with your interests and aptitudes and to reach the maturity—often called emotional intelligence—that defines professionalism. Professionalism requires a high level of maturity and self-awareness of our strengths and frailties.

Self-awareness is only the first half of developing empathy, maturity and emotional intelligence; the second half is developing the discipline needed to avoid self-destructive impulses and habits to get the better of us. The skills of self-management are needed to guide our growth as human beings and our professional pursuit of mastery.

To take one ubiquitous example: responding to criticism. Since we all have egos, we are all prone to responding defensively to criticism. But in terms of professionalism, it is the honest critique that we should be most grateful for, as we cannot improve our skills without trustworthy feedback. If we are unable to recognize honest critiques as a great gift, we have lost a golden opportunity to grow. The surest way to stagnate as a person and professional is to lash out at honest criticism or alienate the person who is willing to help us.

Accepting criticism is not easy for most of us. I can recall every time I was critiqued by someone I respected, as I learned extremely valuable lessons from their criticism. As a young man, I once showed up late and unprepared for a community group meeting I was chairing. An elderly gentleman with immense life experience in a variety of countries dressed me down with some heat for wasting other people's time. I was deeply chastened and never forgot the lesson learned: not being prompt is wasting others' time. Not being prepared is unprofessional and also a waste of others' time. This was an unpaid position, but it didn't matter—I'd acted unprofessionally.

Later in my 20s, when my partner and I were running our construction company, I yelled at an older worker for mishandling some materials. Livid, he took me aside and chewed me out for assigning him responsibility for other workers' faults. Realizing I was in the wrong, I apologized. Once again, my behavior had been unprofessional, and I never forgot the lesson: if emotions get the better of you, apologize quickly and sincerely and don't let it happen again.

When I began writing fiction, I gave a copy of my draft to a professional writer/editor for her review. Confident in my abilities, I expected glowing praise but instead received a very honest critique: my draft was poorly written and flawed on multiple levels. Though my feelings were hurt, this revelation helped me become a better writer in ways that a sugar-coated (and ultimately dishonest) critique could never do.

One key aspect of self-awareness is the ability to put yourself in others' shoes, to see the situation from their perspective. This is essential to responding appropriately and professionally.

For reasons that are unclear since I claim no expertise in such matters, many young people write me asking for advice on career choices. Being sympathetic to their situation, I take time out of my demanding schedule to respond to their questions. Although I don't keep a record of these emails, I cannot recall a single instance where the young person acknowledged my email or thanked me for taking the time to respond.

It would take less than a minute to type, "I really appreciate you taking the time to answer my questions, thank you," but apparently this modest courtesy is beyond these youthful correspondents.

Conversations with other web entrepreneurs confirmed that this experience is not unique to me; others have simply given up responding to such requests because they so rarely receive acknowledgement.

The odds that I would ever hire any of these correspondents or invite them into my network are zero, as they clearly lack the ability to recognize another person's effort on their behalf and have demonstrated a complete lack of professional courtesy. The lesson here is that every communication is an opportunity to accredit yourself. How would you like it if you sacrificed valuable time to respond to someone's request, and that person couldn't even be bothered to acknowledge your effort on their behalf? Being able to put yourself in the shoes of those you interact with is a fundamental part of professionalism, emotional intelligence and self-awareness.

How does one develop self-management? *Do the thing and you shall have the power*. Organize one's time and day as if you were self-employed, even if you're currently jobless; put yourself in the other person's shoes during every encounter, set professional standards for your conduct, habits, processes and responses, and set equally high goals for learning, productivity and effectiveness. Use both accomplishments and failures to add to your store of self-knowledge. Be equally forgiving of your own frailties and the frailties of others. Maintain a positive view of your chances to contribute to your own fulfillment and the effectiveness of other people, enterprises and groups in the pursuit of what interests you.

The process of accrediting yourself can help uncover interests and aptitudes, as completing real-world projects will reveal the depth of your interest in the work. If you find that completing the project has no appeal, this is evidence that there is a mismatch between the task and your personality and/or interests.

The ideal career is doing work that you pursue in your spare time because it's endlessly interesting. Accrediting yourself will help identify work that fits your personality type—for example, whether you prefer to work alone on detail-oriented tasks or whether you prefer to work in a dynamic environment of constant social interactions.

Do the thing and you shall have the power. Though career-counseling and personality exercises can aid our self-discovery, there is no substitute for actually doing the work you think you may like. Completing real-world projects also gives you an opportunity to hone your professionalism and self-management skills.

In today's competitive economy, those whose interests and personalities align with their work will outperform those with little interest in the work other than the security of a paycheck. The accredit yourself process will help identify endeavors where you will be more successful and fulfilled and those that aren't a good match and where you are less likely to be competitive.

Clarifying What Money and Success Mean to You

One poorly understood and rarely mentioned aspect of self-knowledge is being aware of what money and success mean to you. This may seem obvious—we all want more money and greater success—but these beliefs are complex and have a great deal to do with our financial well-being and our day-to-day happiness.

You probably know someone who has achieved a lot in their life but who discounts their success because it doesn't measure up to their impossibly lofty expectations. You also probably know someone who makes a lot of money but who is always broke and hasn't been able to acquire any meaningful financial assets. The first person is unhappy and the second person is anxious, for reasons totally of their own making.

There are a great many reasons why we sabotage ourselves in these ways, and it is beyond the scope of this book to explore that field of human psychology.

Many people define success as having a high-status job and owning status symbols. Once they achieve these goals, they often discover these accomplishments are devoid of meaning, as they were based not on personal fulfillment but on displaying signifiers to gain the approval of others. This realization often leads to personal crisis and a change in career and goals.

Our beliefs about money are often hidden in subconscious patterns that affect our financial decisions in ways we don't fully understand. Thus someone might wonder why they're still financially insecure despite their high salary, and ignore their self-destructive spending habits that are obvious to everyone in their circle.

Pursuing definitions of success that are not really our own leads to frustration and unhappiness; how could somebody else's idea of success possibly be our own?

If we define success not just in terms of status, income or wealth but in our own fulfillment and day-to-day happiness, we have to explore what kind of work we actually enjoy doing every day. Knowing this will greatly improve the chances of success and fulfillment.

The Value of Authenticity in an Inauthentic World

I described the alienation of work and the substitution of intrinsically inauthentic consumerism for authentic meaning at the end of Section Two in *Alienation and Work*. One aspect of self-knowledge that is rarely discussed because it doesn't fit into the conventional view that *increasing consumption increases happiness*.

Our culture has two answers for the question "what is the meaning of life?": work and consumption.

But if the vast majority of work is alienating, as Marx and Lasch held, and those without work have lost the opportunity to establish meaning, as Hoffer maintained, we understand why so few people exhibit evidence of fulfillment and happiness: most Americans claim to be happy but their poor mental and physical health belies this claim.

Consumerism is supposed to generate endless happiness, but what it actually generates is endless derangement and insecurity, as no amount of possessions, status, recognition or fame can turn the inauthentic into the authentic.

What can we do if conventional work and consumerism have little meaning?

We can start by being true to our authentic selves rather than pursuing someone else's dreams.

We can seek to own the means of production (our human and social capital) and the rewards of that production, eliminating the inherent alienation of performing interchangeable work for interchangeable companies and agencies.

If work generates little meaning in our lives, we can seek meaning outside of work in activities and networks that engage and nurture our best selves. For some people, this means spending time with their children, engaging in volunteer activities and pursuing creative endeavors. For others, it's gardening or building things of beauty and utility.

There are many definitions of authenticity; here are two *pointers to authenticity*:

>   1.   What an individual *owns lock, stock and barrel within themselves*, i.e. whatever is present that does not depend on outside acknowledgement.
>
>   2.   Whatever an individual does when left to their own devices that gives them an innate sense of satisfaction that is not dependent on others' confirmation, and during which time passes quickly because the individual is absorbed in the activity.

The programming that we should measure ourselves against others and conform to conventional definitions of success is embedded very deep in our minds. We can even say that the goal of socialization is to instill this conformity to economic and cultural norms.

When I graduated from university, the school's counselor recommended that I go to law school because I had the grades to do so. Instead I pursued what interested me, which was learning how to build houses and writing. In my 30s, I was deeply oppressed by thoughts that I'd done poorly financially because I hadn't done more with my academic abilities, i.e. gone to law school or pursued a PhD.

At some point in my early 40s, it dawned on me that such thoughts were ungrounded in reality; the truth was I had no interest in practicing law and would never have any such interest. If I had pursued someone else's goals, I would have only made myself unhappy by ignoring my authentic interests.

A common bit of career advice is to pursue a high-paying, high-status job because the financial security will enable you to pursue the interests that give your life meaning.

I find this advice flawed on four counts.

>   1.   In a rapidly changing economy, the promised financial security may be illusory. If a law degree leads to a job paying $40,000 a year rather than $170,000 a year, very little security will have been gained, given the decades of student loan payments that

typically accompany law school.

2.	What if the cost of this security is daily misery? Was the cost worth the sacrifice? If happiness (i.e. self-actualization) is the goal of life, then what sense does it make to sacrifice happiness for a financial security that supposedly enables the pursuit of happiness? Why not just pursue meaning and happiness right out of the gate?

3.	Our culture is incapable of pricing the loss of authenticity, so the assumption that financial security is worth any sacrifice is unsupported.

4.	Few that offer this advice disclose that the vast majority of high-status, high-salary jobs tend be demanding and all-consuming, so there is precious little time or energy left to pursue anything else.

I do not mean to discount financial security. Some level of financial security makes life much easier than no financial security. The point here is that the ideal livelihood is one that enables and nurtures your authentic self, not one that sacrifices authenticity and happiness in a single-minded pursuit of financial security.

This is not an either/or choice; it is a balancing act. The goal is not an unattainable perfection of authenticity, security and meaning; the goal is a set of skills that enable *enough security*, a way of life that enables *enough opportunity* to build human and social capital and work that provides *enough meaning*.

The goal is to avoid sacrificing authenticity for a meaningless chimera.

The Difference between Familiarity and Mastery

Familiarity with a field and mastery both create value and aid in solving problems. Having a working understanding of accounting and project management, for example, helps us make a realistic assessment of the overall situation and enables us to better organize resources. Mastery—thorough knowledge of a field and long practice in solving problems within it—generates a different premium.

We explained why this is so in Section Two: if the solution to a problem is not yet known, the work cannot be automated/commoditized. Work that is not tradable or reducible to processes that can be automated generates a premium.

Consider the case of an experienced handyperson who can troubleshoot and repair a variety of different problems. The hand tools needed to perform the vast majority of these repair/maintenance tasks are mass-produced and relatively inexpensive. The financial capital needed to create value as a handyperson is modest; the largest capital expense is transport to various jobs.

By themselves, these tools cannot possibly create any economic value or premium; they are useless. In the hands of an inexperienced worker, they will more likely be a force of value destruction rather than value creation. *Only in the hands of an experienced worker can the tools create value.*

The somewhat-knowledgeable handyperson will lack the experience and skills to quickly and correctly assess the problem and determine the lowest-cost, most efficient means to repair the problem. The less experienced worker may well take ten times as long to make the repair as a master handyperson, and may well select repair options that cost more and are less effective.

In other words, mastery—deep expertise based on experience and *ownership of the work*—is the key element to value creation.

Mastery is not just a mix of knowledge, expertise and experience: it also requires *ownership of the work*, meaning that the master performs all work as if he owns every aspect of it: the process, the final product and the reputation that arises from the results of the work.

The worker who has knowledge and expertise but is incapable of owning their work can never achieve mastery.

It is vital that we understand that mastery is not just a collection of hard skills; it is also a value system of ownership of all work, no matter how menial or trivial it may appear to the outsider.

To illustrate the mindset of mastery, let's consider garden maintenance as an example. The master gardener treats each of the yards in his care as if he owned it, and as if every aspect of his care is a reflection of his reputation and skill. It doesn't matter if the garden's owner is rich or poor or pleasant or unpleasant; the work is done equally well for all because the master gardener owns all his or her work.

In traditional economies, mastery is gained by serving a long unpaid apprenticeship with a master craftsperson. The master often owns his/her own workshop, kitchen, lab, etc., and provides the apprentices with room and board. In exchange for years of hard labor, the master teaches the apprentices the processes and skills of the craft. Such apprentice-master craftsperson arrangements still exist in the traditional handcrafts of Japan.

How does one acquire mastery? There are three interconnected, reinforcing ways:

1.   Self-learning, i.e. when the student is the teacher

2.   Help/instruction from a mentor/master of the trade

3.   Practice, i.e. completing real-world projects that solve problems or create value

Self-Learning to Mastery

We assume that everyone who attended school has learned how to learn, but this is not necessarily true. What we learned in school was how to learn by following instructions. The ability to teach ourselves, to *self-learn to mastery*, is a separate skill that we have to learn on our own.

In the classroom setting, the curriculum is structured so learning is accretive, that is, new learning builds on previous lessons. Self-learning must also be structured to be accretive.

Do the thing and you shall have the power, advised Ralph Waldo Emerson, and this is what we observe in self-learners: they are itching to gain the powers of applied knowledge and practical skills.

Learning is not a smooth curve; it is inherently bumpy, and certain phases of the learning process may be so difficult that even motivated students may become discouraged. These are the critical points where outside resources such as mentors and peers can provide guidance and encouragement.

There are two basic methods that help the self-learning student over these rough spots:

1.   Collaborate with peers pursuing the same goal

2.   Develop mentor-apprentice relationships

The African proverb aptly describes the dual nature of self-learning to mastery: "If you want to walk fast, walk alone. If you want to walk far, walk together." Individual study and practice is the core of self-learning to mastery. Nobel laureate Herbert Simon (Economic Sciences, 1978) summarized this key characteristic of learning: *"Learning results from what the student does and thinks and only from what the student does and thinks."*

Intense, focused study and concentrated work on problem-solving projects build knowledge and skills quickly: this is the equivalent of walking alone and walking fast.

But when the self-learner hits a wall, or needs encouragement, then developing mentors and peer collaborators enables learning over the long haul, i.e. walking together.

The first critical point where help from peers or mentors may be needed is in the initial learning curve. Beginners may be discouraged by their lack of initial progress. Once they've gained the confidence provided by successfully completing the first step, they are better prepared to endure a learning curve in which rewards may be few and far between.

Some skills are inherently difficult and the initial learning curve is very steep, for example, learning to play a musical instrument such as guitar or learning to write software code.

To advance requires self-discipline, time management and a number of other aspects of the eight essential skills. Without self-discipline and an accretive structure that builds on previous lessons, learning is piecemeal and cannot develop the ultimate skill of *self-learning to mastery*.

In the Asian tradition, the neophyte apprentice spends the first few years of apprenticeship doing low-skill, repetitive tasks to learn both self-discipline and the basics of the tradecraft. The objective is threefold:

1. To impress upon the student that the knowledge and skills being passed down to him are highly valued and cannot be gained easily;

2. To guide the student to the experience of mastery in the most basic skills of the trade; and

3. To instill self-discipline and the ability to persevere despite the rewards (empowerment, higher social standing, money) being slim to non-existent.

In other words, the objective is to teach the student that mastery of the trade can only be gained by rigorously following a structured series of accretive steps. Though it is tempting to think one can leapfrog from a few hastily-learned basics to near-mastery, this is the path to failure: each step in the trade must be mastered before it is possible to advance to the next. The master imposes this discipline not as punishment but as the necessarily rigorous path to mastery.

The authority of the mentor-master is not enforced by the government or an institution; rather, the authority flows solely from the mastery and the willingness to teach apprentices. These two traits are the source of the respect given to masters by their peers and apprentices.

This philosophy and program of learning is also the foundation of all martial arts instruction: there can be no mastery without rigorous adherence to strict rules of conduct and incessant practice of a highly structured series of accretive steps--deliberate, dedicated time spent focusing on improving one's skills. This is the core process of gaining mastery, and the ability to self-learn to mastery is a core skill needed to establish and earn a livelihood in today's economy.

Once the student has experienced learning as a process of *accretive, structured steps* that when pursued with self-discipline leads to the *experience of mastery,* he or she has gained the foundational skills of self-learning and the self-confidence to apply them to new fields.

Peers and mentors can help us along the way, but in an economy with few opportunities to establish traditional mentor-apprenticeship relationships, the self-learner must develop a network of peers and mentors who can help at critical junctures in the learning process— what we might term an *ecosystem of collaboration.*

These networks can help in three ways:

1.   Provide solutions to problems that are blocking our progress.

2.   Give us a motivational boost when we're discouraged.

3.   Help us structure our learning plan to be accretive and result in mastery of the subject.

Resources for the Student as Teacher

Learning on one's own is often referred to as self-taught, but perhaps the more accurate description is *the student is also the teacher.* This term covers self-learning and students teaching each other. Books have always given us the means to learn on our own, but now online courses and tutorials have greatly expanded the tools of self-learning. What I call the *University of YouTube* offers tutorials and short video lessons on everything from sewing on a button to electronics design.

Peer-to-peer collaborative learning is similarly untethered from the factory model of Higher Education; it can occur online or in a workshop or under a tree.

What is necessary is a structured course of study and an infrastructure that enables and encourages collaboration, i.e. an *ecosystem of collaboration.*

Careers in today's economy are increasingly an interconnected ecosystem of collaboration rather than a narrowly defined job within a hierarchy. Even within conventional careers, traditional areas of knowledge are spilling over and overlapping with previously distinct fields of expertise, requiring new levels of collaboration.

There are a number of different aspects to *the student is also the teacher.*

Collaboration occurs in two overlapping ecosystems: in person and online. While we often collaborate with the same people in both areas, the two systems are not interchangeable and require slightly different skills and structures.

Peer-to-peer collaboration and teaching is now possible via digital media, for example online forums and tutorials, though this augments rather than replaces collaboration in real-world settings.

Technology has broadened the opportunities for the student to become the teacher via software-enabled adaptive learning. Anecdotally, developing-world students given appropriately programmed tablet computers (basic models now cost about $45) can learn subjects on their own by playing preprogrammed educational games without any teacher at all.

In other words, in areas where teachers are unaffordable or scarce, cheap tablet computers and well-devised games and exercises provide learning for the cost of recharging the batteries.

Since the cost of reproducing and distributing digital lessons is essentially zero, an ever-widening spectrum of instructional videos offers each student a range of teaching approaches and methods which traverse the same material by different pathways.

A great many college-level massively open online courses (MOOCs) are also available for free or for a modest fee. Individual students can review and then select the coursework and approach within the MOOC and YouTube University spheres that is "best of class" for their learning style and aptitudes.

The challenge facing the student-as-teacher is to select a series of courses that lead to mastery.

The number of courses and tutorials is so large that it is daunting to design a series of courses aimed at a specific goal. This is where a mentor or more advanced peer can help by recommending a series of lessons or a pathway of tutorials that will take us to our goal of mastery.

Learning on our own is only one piece of achieving mastery (which is itself only one piece of accrediting yourself). There are two other pieces of mastery: assembling an *ecosystem of collaboration* i.e. a network of mentors and peers and finding real-world problems to solve that give us an opportunity to put our skills and knowledge into practice.

All three pieces work together. How do we find and recruit mentors and peers? We start with a specific field of endeavor/study and then find real-world problems to solve for groups, organizations and enterprises. The process of solving real problems for real organizations will aid the assembly of ecology of collaboration which will then aid the selection of appropriate student-as-teacher coursework.

The process is not linear; it is an interactive model with feedback loops from each piece to every other piece. The choice of project/problem helps define the coursework/learning and the recruitment of mentors and peers.

Entrepreneurial Skills

If we had to summarize the eight essential skills, we might start with *continuous learning and adaptability.* We might also add *entrepreneurial skills*, but *entrepreneurial* is so over-used and poorly defined that the word requires some description to be meaningful.

Entrepreneurial skills in my definition mean:

1. Professionalism (i.e. practicing the eight essential skills)
2. Owning your work
3. Being self-motivated

Entrepreneurism boils down to these three points; all other attributes are part of being professional, owning your work and being self-motivated.

Maintaining Motivation

One key component of self-learning is maintaining self-motivation and self-discipline.

The implicit assumption of conventional pedagogy is that students must be constantly motivated by teachers to learn. This reflects the inherent weaknesses of the Factory Model of Education rather than human nature, as our minds are hard-wired to continuously refine our knowledge and skillsets.

The Factory Model doesn't lend itself to sustaining motivation; indeed, the assembly-line factory model pioneered by Henry Ford in the early 20th century was so unpopular with workers that many quit after a few days. The only motivator that improved the abysmal worker-retention rate was significantly increasing the pay to overcome the workers' natural resistance to mind-numbingly boring hard labor.

We should not be surprised that the Factory Model of Education has failed for many of the same reasons.

Studies of adults pursuing challenging long-term goals such as weight loss find that self-discipline and motivation are not enough, even within the cohort who graduated from college. Rather, these studies find collaboration and peer support is the one predictive factor in maintaining weight loss.

Assuming that students watching Factory Model MOOC courses at home can learn the eight essential skills, achieve mastery and apply these skills in the real world is a fatally flawed assumption. Real-world collaboration and mentor/peer support is an essential part of achieving mastery and accrediting yourself.

To nurture motivation, we first must understand its sources. There are a number of innate sources of motivation: our natural curiosity, for example, leads to learning. Learning practical skills is also inherently empowering, as acquiring new skills boosts our self-confidence and position in the economic hierarchy. This drive for self-betterment is a key source of motivation and self-discipline.

What motivates people to become their own teacher, i.e. to self-learn? As a general rule, their motivation springs from a desire to learn how to do a specific task or solve a specific problem.

One basic way to maintain motivation is to design a series of accretive tasks or projects that are small enough to be manageable and that build on previous lessons and projects. Trying to tackle an enormous field of knowledge all at once is overwhelming, so breaking mastery into small steps is essential to maintaining motivation. Completing each small step is rewarding, even if progress on the entire project appears modest.

Willpower is also a key part of motivation. *Do the thing and you shall have the power* requires the willpower to get started. But willpower has a dual nature: on the one hand, it is a finite resource; we do not have unlimited reserves of willpower, so we must conserve it for the most critical tasks. On the other hand, willpower increases with practice: the more you exercise willpower, the more you have.

Willpower is like a muscle: overuse leads to exhaustion, but regular use leads to expanded capacity.

We covered using willpower to mold new productive habits in Section Three, *Investing in Ourselves.*

Setting goals is the third essential to maintaining motivation: without an overarching goal—achieving mastery and applying the eight essential skills—it's easy to lose our way and become distracted.

So maintaining motivation requires these four components:

1. Overarching goals that organize and prioritize our daily efforts (achieving mastery and the eight essential skills)

2. Investing our willpower to cement new habits that further our goals

3. Breaking down every problem or project into its constituent parts, i.e. *bite-sized* manageable steps that can be completed with available resources.

4. Collaborate with others, i.e. establish an ecology/network of collaboration that supports our goals and efforts.

Collaboration is a two-way street: helping others also motivates us to stay engaged and to learn more so we can help others more.

Joining Ecologies of Collaboration

Recruiting mentors and peers who can help us learn new skills is a daunting task when starting from zero. We have a powerful ally in this, however: many people find it rewarding to help others. We want to share what we have learned, and I call this web-enabled movement *the philanthropy of knowledge.* This broad-based philanthropic generosity feeds a continuously expanding and entirely free library we can tap, much of it online.

People within a field, community or trade are already communicating and collaborating with each other in *ecologies of collaboration;* plugging into these existing networks is much easier than building your own from scratch —though sometimes that becomes necessary if the purpose of the network is new.

There are three core dynamics in *ecologies of collaboration*:

1.   *Reciprocity*—giving as well as taking

2.   The *strength of weak ties* –it's the size of the network that matters, not the strength of each tie within it

3.   *Ecologies of collaboration* you join become part of your social capital

I use the word *ecology* rather than network because I think it more accurately describes the complexity and interactions of collaborating. The word *network* implies nodes of roughly equal strength, rather like membership in a club, while *networking* has been degraded by over-use to mean establishing a weak link to someone you don't know in a brief encounter or online network.

Network implies a static passive array through which messages or signals pass. *Ecology* implies a much more dynamic mix of symbiosis, competition within niches, food chains and a spectrum of creatures and biota large and small.

The other key word is *collaboration*: what you seek is connections that enable you to find people you can collaborate with as peers, mentors, clients, employers, employees and co-workers.

The key to building social capital is *reciprocity*—you're not just looking to get something, you're looking for a chance to contribute. *Collaboration* implies mutual benefit, the key to social capital.

I mentioned the *strength of weak ties* in Section Four, *Massively Networked Participants Fuel Innovation*. Here's what the concept means: those who share *strong ties* (close friends and family members, for example) already share the same information. This is why asking close friends and family members if they know of any job openings usually yields no results—

everyone in the circle already knows the same information, so if there was a job opening known to the circle, you would also already know it.

The most productive networks are those that link to the broadest range of information, knowledge, and experience. Narrow expertise and limited circles of contacts severely limit problem-solving the knowledge available to the network is limited. Interconnected circles of people joined by weak ties include a much larger body of knowledge and expertise.

We can visualize this concept by drawing three circles: the first small circle is our close friends, the second larger one is our friends' friends, and the third and largest circle is our friends' friends' friends. Our ties to our friends' friends are weak, and those to people in the third circle are weaker still. Nonetheless the knowledge in that large third circle is still available to us via *the strength of weak ties*.

The insights provided by this principle suggest that the most productive way to assemble a network of peers, mentors and collaborators is to join circles that are connected to other circles that have no connections to the ones you currently inhabit.

How do massively networked circles of people fuel innovation? They actively match problem-solvers to problems that need to be solved.

Ecologies of collaboration typically have a range of participants. Some might be specialists; others might not be very active while a few become *super-users*, the human equivalent of network routers that are linked to many more nodes than average users and who route more communication and information than less connected members. These are the most influential people in the network (and here I am referring to ecologies of collaboration) because they do the most. Ecologies of collaboration are informal and *self-organizing do-ocracies*, meaning that they are not hierarchical: super-users become influential by doing more.

The goal for new members of any network of collaboration is to identify the super-users with the most connections and the most influence. These are the people who will have heard of problems that need problem-solvers, for example, you. If you need help figuring out a difficult task, they will likely be able to recommend someone who is willing to help you.

Your first communication with a super-user should be to volunteer to help on projects that need participants. The more you do, the more you will learn and the greater your influence in the network. The most valuable people in any self-organizing ecology are: super-users, specialists who can solve particularly knotty or rare problems, and *go-to guys/gals*, people who can solve a variety of problems with minimal fuss and few resources. As a beginner, it will take time to become a super-user, and you may not yet have high-level skills that make you a specialist. But virtually anyone with the eight skills of professionalism can become a *go-to gal/guy.*

Everyone loves go-to gals/guys because they solve problems without making a financially or emotionally costly production of the task. They take ownership of the task and locate and organize the people and resources to do so. They might ask super-users for suggestions, but they figure out what's needed and organize the people and processes.

If I were 19 years old and on my own again, I would seek out a big group house of the incubator variety, where virtually every resident was an entrepreneur or working for a start-up company, and I would offer myself as the go-to guy for the house in exchange for a place to sleep. Need a meal cooked? I'm on it. Yard tended? Lockset replaced? I'm on it. I would not know how to do many of the tasks, but each task would be small enough to figure out with help from a friend of a resident or a friend of a friend or online tutorials. If I messed the job up because it was my first time, I would have the freedom to re-do it, as nobody would be supervising me except me.

(If I chose to pursue a college education, I would do so in between work, not the other way around, just as I did in my youth.)

Being the go-to gal/guy in such a setting would be an incredibly fast track to building human and social capital very quickly. What better network to plug into than one formed of entrepreneurs who are busy failing fast and failing often?

Our task then is to find ways to plug into existing networks of people who are studying or working in our field of interest. There are many ways to do so: for example, taking a local community college class and seeking projects to collaborate on with other students. Joining a community group is another way to start making connections to wider circles.

The most dynamic parts of the economy—start-ups, co-ops, and other parts of the community economy—are opt-in (i.e. participants freely join, participate and leave) *do-ocracies*, where those who contribute the most tend to accumulate the most influence. Your social capital will expand as you accomplish more in do-ocracy organizations, as those within these organizations know you are directly responsible for solving problems and creating value.

The strength of weak ties works both ways, of course. Your efforts to help someone you don't yet know personally will form weak ties to that person and the circles he/she inhabits, and these weak ties will add innovative problem-solving power to your own network. Aiding others whenever possible is an investment in the power of weak ties to build your own social capital. Not every investment pays off, but the cumulative effect of mentoring and helping others is profound.

Social-media networks are not substitutes for active participation in do-ocracies and organizations where your engagement makes a difference—and others know that you've made a difference.

Actively Seek Problems to Solve

The starting point of accrediting yourself is finding a real-world problem to solve that demonstrates your abilities and skills. Let's start by comparing this process to the conventional job search.

The process of finding problems to solve introduces you to people who may become trusted mentors or peers.

The benefit of volunteering in a community organization is that the people who devote time and energy to such organizations (churches, environmental issues, local sports, etc.) are self-selected doers who generally know many people, some of whom might be able to help you as peers or mentors—the power of weak ties.

The community economy tends to be a *do-ocracy* in which those who contribute the most have the most influence. This is an excellent environment for anyone seeking to make a difference (i.e. solve problems and create value) and make connections to people who might become collaborators, peers and mentors, as doers tend to collaborate with other doers.

Contrast this with the conventional approach, where the student gets a college degree, prepares a resume detailing their coursework and work history and then applies for a series of jobs. The degree and resume are presumed to accredit the graduate's knowledge, skills and readiness to create value for an employer. The employer reviews numerous resumes and interviews graduates, and then selects the one with the most impressive resume and academic performance.

The flaws in this process are readily apparent. A degree and a resume offer minimal evidence of the graduate's soft skills, ability to solve problems, learn on his own and create value. Resumes are seen as a branch of public relations, crafted to place the applicant in the best possible light and pass through all the conventional Human Resource Department's filters.

The process is passive: the graduate plays a numbers game based on probabilities, i.e. if I send out 100 resumes I will get five interviews and if I get five interviews I will get one job offer.

But experience suggests this probabilities-based approach no longer works: many graduates have sent out hundreds of resumes and applications and not received a single response, much less a job offer.

This conventional process is miles away from the practical approach of directly accrediting your knowledge, skills, values and problem-solving abilities within ecologies of collaboration.

Graduates face a chicken-egg problem: employers want work experience, but how do you get experience if no one will hire you due to lack of experience? The answer is to go out in the real world and seek problems to solve within organizations and enterprises.

This is not as difficult as it may appear at first glance. Let's start with the basic sectors of the economy: the state (government), private enterprise and the community economy, my terms for every organization and activity that is neither funded by the state nor organized around the goal of making a profit. This includes churches (by which I mean all houses of worship) and a wide spectrum of community groups.

Each sector has formal positions that are difficult to obtain. But each sector also has less formal parts where volunteers can make a difference. In government, this includes city agencies; in private enterprise, this includes many small businesses and start-ups, and in the community economy, this includes a wide spectrum of local groups and organizations.

A great many community groups and organizations lack proper accounting and public relations programs, due to limited staffing, funding and expertise. Finding a problem to solve that fits your interests and field of endeavor may be as easy as walking into local churches, environmental organizations, neighborhood groups, volunteer-based sports programs or any one of hundreds of other community-economy organizations and asking what projects need doing or problems that need solving.

The list is generally be long enough and varied enough that the willing volunteer can find something that aligns with their field of interest and goals of mastery. Data entry, bookkeeping, and public relations (social media, outreach to members, contacting local media, etc.) are often unmet needs/problems that need to be solved.

Completing these projects (or organizing a system that will outlast your own participation) creates value for the organization. This is what employers hire people to do: solve problems and create value. This is the goal of offering one's services—not just to donate time but to identify serious problems that you can solve and *document to accredit your abilities and experience.*

Starting this search for problems to solve/value to create while you are enrolled in a class is ideal, as people are naturally inclined to help students and to view them as a potential resource. If you want to get into financial services, for example, if you contact small investment management firms asking for work you will likely be told there are no openings. If you contact these same firms as a student asking for some guidance from an established expert in the field, you will likely be invited to meet with the owner or key staff.

In the meeting, your inquiries should focus on identifying the key problems of the business—problems that limit expansion, profitability, retention of clients, etc. People might hesitate to speak openly about such problems with job applicants, but they are more likely to be honest with a student who is seeking to understand the business as part of a research project.

If you are out of school, then launch an independent study project that serves the same goal. *Do the thing and you shall have the power.* If you're interested in investment management, start managing an imaginary portfolio as if it were real client money. Learn everything you can about portfolio management, risk management, etc.—the constituent parts of investment management—and then share your conclusions with small investment management firms and ask for feedback.

In my case, this led to my meeting a sole proprietor investment manager who desperately needed an office manager but did not recognize the need or know how to go about hiring one. The essential systems of his business (and indeed, of any business)—information technology (IT), accounting, data analysis of his investment returns, reports to clients, marketing, etc.—were all in various stages of collapse due to rising complexity, subcontractors leaving or simple abandonment. Even though my college degree was in philosophy, a field unrelated to investment management or financial services, it was clear to him that my interest in the field was sincere and already well-developed, and that I could solve problems.

As a result, a business owner who was not even sure what he needed or how to hire the person he needed to save his business ended up hiring me to rebuild his firm's back-office systems. A company with no job openings ended up hiring someone fulltime at a reasonably competitive salary, and the person with no formal experience or training in investment management gained an experienced, knowledgeable mentor.

To be productive, I had to learn an enormous amount about the business and the failing core accounting, management and reporting systems in a short time. This was stressful but well worth the effort, as I gained a set of skills that could be applied to other businesses, not just in that sector but in every field.

I stayed on about a year and half, enough time to set up a suite of systems that would serve the enterprise in a sustainable, productive fashion and help my boss find the ideal person to replace me. What made my replacement ideal was not her resume, but her grasp of the eight essential skills. She stayed with the company until the owner passed away 15 years later—a sad day for all of us who worked for him and with him over the years.

Whatever field of endeavor you have chosen to master, reach out to enterprises, groups and organizations that might benefit from your interest and desire to solve their most pressing problems.

Contacting a variety of community groups and small enterprises will give you a feel for the range of problems that organizations need solved and also introduce unexpected connections and pathways to your goal of mastery and self-accreditation.

For example, someone who wants to gain construction/building skills might naturally start by contacting builders and contractors. But more than likely they will encounter the same difficulties mentioned above—a lack of credentials and experience. A more likely way to gain experience might be to ask local churches if you can help with any building maintenance projects, since virtually every older building has maintenance issues that require a range of construction skills. Whoever is handling the maintenance will likely welcome a motivated volunteer, and that person will likely offer connections to others in the field.

My own experience in community groups taught me that the number of tasks awaiting a go-to-gal/guy is truly enormous. Newsletters need to be written and distributed, grant proposals written and pitched, mailing lists culled and updated, subcommittees formed—all of which can certify your abilities, leadership and professionalism in a variety of other fields and jobs.

Innovation and problem-solving often depend not just on narrow expertise but on networks, cross-pollination of disciplines and a variety of experiences. Learn to use the networks that already exist in organizations to help solve problems, and use the power of weak ties to deepen your social capital.

This process of helping a community group, city program or enterprise solve critical problems naturally introduces you to key participants and contributors in those organizations. Once these people see that you actually complete projects that create value and are able to collaborate effectively with others, they will naturally be disposed to offer you whatever help they can in widening your network of peers, mentors potential employers or people who might introduce you to potential employers.

Tackling problems or projects for an organization does three things simultaneously. It directs your course of learning as you seek the knowledge, skills and contacts needed to solve the problem, it gives you real-world experience in problem-solving and collaborating with others, and it introduces you to a widening circle of people who will help you assemble an ecology of collaboration, i.e. a network of knowledgeable peers and mentors who can accredit your knowledge, accomplishments, values and skills.

It's important to remember that though others can assist you or offer guidance, real learning only comes from what you do yourself. The quote from Herbert Simon encapsulates this truth: *"Learning results from what the student does and thinks and only from what the student does and thinks."*

Documenting and Sharing Your Completed Projects

The documentation phase of accrediting yourself is a four-step process:

1. Document the project you contributed to or completed as if you were a reporter, with a synopsis or summary, quotes from participants, photos and a brief description

2.   Recruit others you worked with to verify your role

3.   Post this documentation online where others can easily access it

4.   Distribute the site to your collaborators and appropriate networks within your field of interest

The key to Step 1 is to understand the difference between journalistic reporting, which strives to be objective and verifiable, and resume-type marketing, which has been edited for promotional purposes.

Report the project as if you worked for the media. Keep in mind that your peers and mentors will be reading the report; list all participants and give credit where credit is due. Letting others shine reflects confidence and leadership.

Since our culture expects everyone to be an advocate, the temptation is to exaggerate our abilities and contributions, and to inflate modest accomplishments into unrealistically grandiose achievements.

Remember to put yourself in the shoes of a prospective employer or client; they don't want the glossy, heavily edited public-relations version, they want a description of what problems arose and how they were resolved.

Remember that the real work is done not by setting goals but by establishing and perfecting cost-effective, productive processes. If you took over a group's mailing list and newsletter production for example, don't just document the steps you took (updating the mailing list, switching the newsletter to a more attractive template, etc.): document the process of collaboration ("After meeting with the executive director and the outreach committee, I drew up a proposal to make the newsletter a tool to recruit new members and not just report on activities"), how you assessed what wasn't working well/needed to be fixed and your proposed *systemic* solution.

In other words, the solution wasn't just a one-time updating of the group's mailing list; your solution was to make a well-thought out collaborative assessment of the entire process of producing and distributing the newsletter, and asking if the newsletter was truly serving the core needs of the group.

This process culminated in your proposed systemic solution, i.e. a clearly documented process that someone after you could follow to produce the newsletter without having to reinvent the wheel.

Various obstacles invariably arise in the course of any project, and how you overcome obstacles, objections, conflicts, errors, etc. will be of keen interest to prospective employers and clients, as this documents your problem-solving and professional abilities.

If you are learning cabinetry, then scan the preliminary sketches provided by the owner, any working drawings you prepared of the new cabinet, your materials list and cost projection, photos of your basic assembly process and photos of the finished cabinet.

Remember that this documentation is evidence of your ability to communicate clearly and succinctly. Professionals don't want to read an over-written graduate thesis—they want a simple, well-organized journalistic-style report: who, what, when, where, what problems arose, how they were solved, how the organization/client gained from the completed project.

The Chinese sage Lao-Tzu wrote, *the journey of a thousand miles starts with a single step.* The process of documenting your contributions may proceed slowly or haltingly, but the value accumulates with each project. Your first project may not look overly impressive, but ten such projects will reflect all the qualities employers, collaborators and clients value: professionalism, perseverance, leadership, ability to learn on your own, problem-solving, value creation, communication, and ability to collaborate effectively with others.

Soliciting Third-Party Verification and Testimonials

In a world saturated with marketing, hucksterism and self-serving spin, we have all developed highly tuned skepticism detectors to identify hype, nonsense, exaggerations, fakes and lies. The primary filtering tool enabled by the web is third-party reviews posted on sites such as Yelp, where other users and customers post their experience and opinion.

In the old model of media, a newspaper or magazine would employ one knowledgeable critic to review films, book, restaurants, art exhibits, etc., and the reviewer's expertise lent credibility to the review.

In new media, people rely not on one critic's opinion but on the crowd-sourced consensus of dozens or hundreds of other users/customers. While one individual may have an axe to grind or a bias that slants their perception of a film, café, etc., the motivations of hundreds of users are filtered out simply by the lack of material gain or influence any one reviewer can accrue.

If an owner of a new café bribes a half-dozen friends or employees to post positive (and exaggerated) reviews to promote the café, real customers will post honest feedback that counters the fake reviews. Sites that post reviews are also keen to filter out gamed reviews, and people who post only one or two reviews are filtered or devalued, as those seeking to game the system rarely bother to laboriously assemble a meaningful portfolio of reviews first.

For these reasons, what you should seek is not recommendations so much as reports of the facts by trustworthy third-parties. If you accomplished goals, finished projects, solved problems and added value, a simple reporting of the facts is testimony of your values, skills and abilities.

What makes a third-party verifiably trustworthy is a wealth of online links that cannot be gamed. For example, a board member of a community group is likely to have served o pother boards or committees, and these links will appear in a web search (sometimes known as "Googling" the person).

Super-users (discussed in *Ecologies of Collaboration*) are most likely to have a variety of easily verifiable links documenting their trustworthiness.

Why does this matter? If someone collects testimonials from friends with few verifiable links or activities, there is no way for a prospective employer or collaborator to verify the testimonial is trustworthy, i.e. isn't exaggerated, faked or gamed. The ideal set of testimonials is provided by people you worked with closely whose own value in various networks is easily verified online.

This is another example of the *strength of weak ties*. The more ties a person has that can be quickly verified as legitimate, the more value their testimonials will have. A short comment such as "This gal is pretty good" from an accomplished, extremely well-connected person is worth more than a long, effusive recommendation from someone whose networks and accomplishments cannot be verified.

If key people are too busy to write a few paragraphs verifying your completed project (as will often be the case—it's nothing personal, it's just that they're over-committed and over-scheduled), write a brief, clearly written report yourself (who, what, where, when, how and the goal accomplished) and ask them to sign it or attach their name to it.

Remember that prospective employers and collaborators want an overview that can be scanned quickly and documentation behind the overview should they want to learn more about the project, your role in it, the problems that arose, etc. They want a report, not a sales pitch, so remember to share credit where credit is due and recognize mentors and those who helped you.

One testimonial from a respected professional will carry more weight than a half-dozen testimonials from unknowns, but as with any other third-party verification system, a wide array of reports (assuming they are legitimate and not faked or gamed) will accumulate into a powerful statement. If you can't get testimonials from well-connected professionals, then get honest reports from as wide a variety of colleagues and collaborators as possible. In other words, build on the strength of weak ties.

Once again, a key strategy is to put yourself in the shoes of the person you hope will look at your blog/website: assume they are well-informed and busy. List the key points in the opening summary, and then provide further details in the narrative and supporting documentation.

If you find a well-organized website, then by all means incorporate what you learned into your own site. Your blog/website should not be a static project that is completed and abandoned; it should constantly be revised, updated and improved to reflect your own advancement.

The Value of a Professional Blog/Website

Many people rely on social media such as Twitter or Facebook to present their public selves, but these formats do not lend themselves to serious, well-organized and professionally presented documentation. Only a website or blog that you completely own and manage can document your professional skills and completed projects.

As with every other aspect of accredit yourself, creating a website to present yourself and your work offers a valuable opportunity to display your communication and design skills. Nothing says "slapdash and unprofessional" like a sloppy blog or website, and nothing says "professional and productive" like a cleanly organized, clearly composed website.

The templates and tools needed to build a simply but professional blog or website are free, and tutorials on how to do so abound. Templates are a starting point, but the first thing anyone looking at your blog/website will notice is whether you have the skills to go beyond a simple template and customize your site to optimally communicate your projects and skillsets.

Your blog or website will have a unique URL (web address) that will enter the collaborative networks you have joined or are developing. Since social media and web-based communication is now core to every enterprise and organization, displaying your working knowledge of web-based media is an important step in accrediting your ability to communicate clearly.

Accreditation and Self-Employment

The process of accrediting your value to prospective employers and accrediting your value to prospective clients is identical. This is how many people become self-employed: someone sees their excellent work and asks them to do the same work for them. Though many people view self-employment as insecure and more responsibility than they care to shoulder, from the point of view of the changing economy, everyone is self-employed: those working for others are simply temporarily lending their self-employment skills to others.

The ideal collaborator is someone who sees no line between employment and self-employment, someone who owns their work regardless of the circumstance. They operate with the same values and ownership whether they are employed by an organization, collaborating with others on a project or are self-employed. This is the ultimate adaptability and thus the ultimate security.

The Goal of Accrediting Yourself: To Be the Only One Who Does What You Do

If we had to summarize the goal in accrediting yourself, we might start by emphasizing the verification of our adaptability, ability to self-learn, professionalism and entrepreneurial skills.

But perhaps the ultimate goal of accrediting yourself was best said by Grateful Dead founder Jerry Garcia: *"You do not merely want to be considered just the best of the best. You want to be considered the only one who does what you do."*

This is a succinct, profound encapsulation of creating value, the matrix of work and the premium of labor: you do not want to demonstrate that you are one of the best in a field; you want to stake out a piece of the emerging economy that is yours alone.

This does not necessarily require an astounding level of accomplishment; it also characterizes a person with a set of experiences and skills that cross-pollinate in unique ways to create value and solve new problems.

Section Six: Putting It All Together

Let's put everything we've learned together in a few final points.

What Is Security?

It is human nature to seek both security and novelty, and on first glance these may appear to be mutually exclusive: security means safe, stable and known, while novelty means change and exposure to the unknown/new.

In state-cartel capitalism, there are three recognized sources of financial security:

1.	Gain access to the spoils system of entrenched Elites (such as Wall Street) via family connections or connections gained through elite universities or other elitist portals

2.	Get hired by sprawling bureaucracies (typically government agencies or government contractors) that are designed to dissipate accountability so that no one can be fired for underperformance, laziness or incompetence

3.	Launch a business that either generates substantial, stable profits or that has new technology that can be sold to a large corporation for an immense gain

In general, the number of opening in the spoils system of entrenched Elites is very limited. Roughly 15% of the workforce (22 million people) work for government at all levels, and millions more work for government contractors that are basically agencies of the state. But since those who value this type of security have self-selected to work for government agencies precisely to obtain this security, the number of openings is largely limited to replacement of retirees.

While many dream of starting a hyper-successful business, relatively few have the financial, human and social capital needed to start and grow such an enterprise.

So what do the rest of us do for security?

Let's start by reviewing what we learned about capitalism and the emerging economy. We found that entrenched Elites and bureaucracies are self-liquidating, meaning that they are organized to respond to diminishing returns by *doing more of what has failed spectacularly*, that is, precisely what created the diminishing returns in the first place.

This is why I describe our dysfunctional, predatory financial system as *Peak Wall Street*: Wall Street's financialization and capture of the political process have reached the top of the S-Curve and will decline, as it has consumed all the available oxygen and has no more room for further expansion.

The same can be said of all the other cartels: pharmaceuticals, national defense, healthcare, higher education, etc.: every cartel has already consumed all the oxygen available in its space and is far down the road of diminishing returns. Every dominant cartel in the system is at the top of the S-Curve, poised for an unexpected and uncontrolled decline.

The more sclerotic, hidebound, inefficient and wasteful the cartel or bureaucracy, the more vulnerable it is to *creative destruction*. The gains will be as outsized as the inefficiencies destroyed.

In other words, the large-scale bureaucracies that appear secure in mid-2014 are less secure than is generally believed.

Nassim Taleb of *Black Swan* fame has explained that jobs characterized by low-intensity volatility and day-to-day insecurity (driving a taxi was his example; I would say any sort of free-lance project-based collaboration) are actually more secure than supposedly secure jobs that come with all sorts of hidden fragilities and systemic dependencies.

This book prepares anyone to navigate do-ocracies that reward adaptability, professionalism and entrepreneurial skills. The cost of this security is day-to-day volatility, dissent and variation, all of which provide the critical information needed to maintain the system's adaptability and vigor.

In other words, *stability breeds failure.*

Embracing the security of bureaucracies and entrenched-interests is actually a bet that creative destruction will magically cease destroying what is inefficient and unproductive, that diminishing returns can continue until the output is less than zero and that bureaucracies and cartels will all magically escape the S-Curve.

Embracing what we're told is insecure—self-employment, project-based collaboration, worker-owned cooperatives, and so on—is actually more secure in a rapidly changing economy.

New models of Ownership, Work and Collaboration

Let's go back to the example of the market for beer in the early 1970s, when consolidation had reached the top of the S-Curve and a handful of corporations owned almost every brewery in the nation. Locally owned breweries were essentially extinct, and microbreweries did not yet exist. The market for locally crafted beer appeared to be zero, and jobs in microbreweries were also zero. Anyone talking about starting a microbrewery at the time would have been discouraged from investing time and money in such a risky venture.

Yet this perception of zero opportunity was exactly backwards: the extreme of corporate consolidation meant the opportunities for microbreweries and making craft beer were unlimited. The apparently stable market dominated by corporations was ripe for creative destruction.

In the same fashion, our economy is dominated by large-scale state agencies and cartels that appear to be stable and impervious to change, much less creative destruction. But these extremes of ownership and control mean the opportunities for new, more productive arrangements are as unlimited as the market for microbreweries in the mid-1970s. But since those new markets and arrangements are not yet well-known, the vast majority of people are unaware of them.

As we have discussed at length, human and social capital are the means of production, and the tools for producing goods and services are falling rapidly in cost, meaning that they are within the grasp of far more people than ever before.

Since doing interchangeable work for interchangeable bureaucracies is intrinsically alienating, and not owning your work or the output of your work is also alienating, the innate human desire for authenticity and fulfillment means those arrangements which reduce alienation will attract the energy and capital of those who cannot bear to sacrifice themselves for an illusory security.

I have mentioned a number of new models for ownership, work and collaboration: worker-owned cooperatives, consumer-owned cooperatives, community-owned resources open to participation by any resident, project-based collaborative arrangements and self-organizing networks that replace hierarchical bureaucracies. The access-based model (as opposed to the ownership model) is also creating opportunities to *do more with less*. The no-middleman model is another alternative that reduces costs and opens new distribution opportunities from producer to end consumer.

We can summarize this alternative view of productive systems with this phrase: *trust the network, not the state or corporation*. The intelligence and creativity of the distributed, opt-in network exceeds that of a centralized hierarchical bureaucracy. *Do-ocracies* are inherently more transparent, adaptable, accessible and democratic than centralized hierarchies.

The other key feature of such alternatives is the workers/participants *own the work and the output*. Work that is alienating when performed for the state or corporation becomes authentic and purposeful when those producing the work own the processes and the output.

The 40-hour a week job working for a single employer is another model that is no longer adaptable enough to fit new arrangements of collaboration. I have written about the *hybrid work* model for years. Hybrid work draws purpose and meaning from a variety of projects and work, some paid, some unpaid, some compensated by value other than money; *hybrid work* generates a mix of income from a variety of sources and investments in yourself. I attribute my own security and work satisfaction to the variety and multiple income streams of my *hybrid work* lifestyle.

Some call this a *patchwork career* of several income streams, perhaps mixing self-employment with multiple sources of paid work. Whatever the name you prefer, the key features of hybrid work are adaptability, flexibility, ownership of work choices, some self-employment/collaborative work and some income from investing in yourself and your own enterprises.

Opportunities are most abundant in sectors not under the control of the centralized state or cartel-corporations: the *do-ocracies* in the community economy and The Degrowth economy, which is focused not on maximizing profit or state control but on sustainability and *doing more with less*. The focus of Degrowth is on living a rewarding life that consumes fewer resources and less money. The Degrowth economy is by default a networked, decentralized, localized *do-ocracy*.

Integrating the Matrix of Work

Let's integrate what we learned about the matrix of work and the premium generated by labor with what we've learned about accrediting yourself: focus on developing skills that are high-touch, non-tradable, and resistant to commoditization and automation. Focus on developing a spectrum of skills that includes utilizing new networks and technologies. Seek skills that create *hybrid vigor*, i.e. skills that can be cross-pollinated to solve new problems. Focus on accrediting these high-value, commoditization-resistant skills.

If you need to develop skills that can generate income right away, focus on acquiring skills that can be learned to mastery in a few months. Once you've reached that plateau, you'll be able to fund the longer-term learning you will need to gain mastery of skills that take years to develop.

From the perspective of the matrix of work, security can be defined as owning a variety of skills, and/or specialized skills that are immune to commoditization. Those with a variety of skills will always be able to create value in some capacity.

Moving to an Infrastructure of Opportunity

Even the most talented, skilled individual will be unable to create value or solve problems if there is no opportunity for his/her skills. Even the hardiest seed cannot grow if it lands on desert hardpan.

This means you may have to move to a place that offers an infrastructure of opportunity, or assemble the infrastructure with like-minded people. Assembling the infrastructure from scratch is difficult and time-consuming, which is why the majority of people who find opportunities extremely limited move to urban zones (cities or large towns) which exist because they offer an infrastructure of opportunity.

Managing Change

"If you do not change direction, you may end up where you are heading." Lao Tzu

Though I haven't discussed this directly, any book about establishing and maintaining a livelihood in a changing economy is also about *managing change.*

Famed psychiatrist Carl Jung proposed that humans use four principal psychological functions to process experience: sensation, intuition, feeling, and thinking. The Myers-Briggs personality test seeks to divide those who predominantly rely on one or two of the functions into various personality types.

In other words, certain personality types may be more deeply impacted by an intellectual insight than others. For example, some people may be predisposed to read about the role of fitness in health and start a fitness program based solely on that knowledge, while others have to experience a heart attack before changing their daily lifestyle habits.

While insight, knowledge and direct experience are all important motivational starting points, the key to transformation is to design a process that brings about the change we want. For example, if we want to improve our health and fitness, we must first design a process that yields the changes we want: an exercise routine and a diet that we can live with in the long-term. A process that doesn't fit our personality is likely to fail: if a person is not a morning person, a plan that requires awakening at 5 a.m. for a jog in darkness is not sustainable.

In a similar way, a creative solution to a problem might suddenly occur to us, but the implementation of that solution typically requires a process.

In everyday life, processes are habits: the process of improving fitness results from fitness routines becoming habits.

We resist change for all sorts of reasons, starting with our innate preference to conserve whatever has worked in the past (*conservation of existing processes*) as trying something new entails risk: the change might yield no gain at all.

But we may also resist making productive changes because the motivators don't activate our personality type. We may want to change but lack the ability to develop a process that yields the desired output (a new habit, a new routine, etc.).

Fortunately, we can learn how to develop processes by studying project management and systems: what process will yield the results we want?

Each of us has a comfort zone of creativity and routines. Studies suggest that pushing ourselves outside of our comfort zones yields new insights. We also know that advances occur when concepts and ideas from one field cross-pollinate knowledge in different fields, a process that leads to *hybrid vigor*.

Managing change is easier if we have self-knowledge about our personality type and if we develop processes that will get us where we want to be, including pushing ourselves out of our comfort zones and developing a wide base of cross-pollinating knowledge that generates new insights and value.

Become the Person Everyone Who Owns the Output Wants to Work With

What kind of person do we want to work with? For most of us, it's someone who is honest, generous, good-natured, forgiving and competent, someone who is a good listener and who communicates clearly, and someone who keeps their own personal troubles out of the workplace.

But if you ask those who *own the output of the work*, for example, everyone in a worker-owned cooperative, the demands are even higher. When the output is everyone's livelihood, what people want is professional ownership of the work and dedication to customers, clients and the quality of the product. They want go-to gals and guys with entrepreneurial skills who get the job done with a minimum of waste. They want people who know how to learn new processes and material efficiently. They want people who can maintain a sense of humor even under stress, people who can maintain a focus on priorities that serve the interests of the group, not just themselves. They want people who ask more of themselves than they ask of anyone else. They want people who can accept honest criticism as a gift rather than an insult. They want people who are able to praise others when praise is due. They want people who seek mastery for the fulfillment and meaning mastery provides. They want professionalism, because professionals get more done in less time and with less waste than non-professionals.

Anyone who can become the person *everyone who owns the output wants to work with* will find work once they join the appropriate ecologies of collaboration and accredit themselves.

www.ingramcontent.com/pod-product-compliance
Lightning Source LLC
Chambersburg PA
CBHW031735150726
47989CB00006B/2473